How To Read A Difficult Book

A Beginner's Guide to the Lost Art of Philosophical Reading

Peter A. Redpath

 Public Philosophy Press

Republished by Public Philosophy Press 2021
Phoenix, Arizona

Copyright © 2021 by Peter A. Redpath
Original Publication 1999 Peter A. Redpath

All rights reserved. No part of this publication may be reproduced, stored or transmitted in any form or by any means, electronic, mechanical, photocopying, recording, scanning, or otherwise without written permission from the publisher. It is illegal to copy this book, post it to a website, or distribute it by any other means without permission.

Cover art by Beth Ellen Nagle

Typesetting by Alyssa Anderson

First edition
ISBN: 978-1-7365424-0-8

DEDICATED

to

Charles Jones and

The George W. Strake, Jr. Foundation

For Their Support of Philosophical Scholarship

TABLE OF CONTENTS

Acknowledgments	i
Foreword	ii
Introduction	iv
Chapter 1 *Learning, Tools, Books, and Philosophical Reading*	1
Chapter 2 *The Skill of Philosophical Reading*	10
Chapter 3 *General Kinds of Books and Kinds of Teaching*	16
Chapter 4 *Philosophical Reading*	20
Chapter 5 *Three Rules for "Philosophically Reading" any Book*	27
Chapter 6 *A Book's General Outline*	41
Chapter 7 *Philosophically Reading Theoretical Matters*	57
Chapter 8 *Philosophically Reading Matters of Measurement*	67
Chapter 9 *Philosophically Reading Practical Matters*	85

Chapter 10
Philosophically Reading Matters of Imaginable Experience   92

Chapter 11
Philosophically Reading Mixed Matters, Conclusion   100

Study and Discussion   106

Notes   126

ACKNOWLEDGMENTS

I thank the American Maritain Association for doing an initial printing of this book, Patrick S. J. Carmack, the Great Books Academy and Socratic Books, for doing a subsequent publication of it; and Curtis L. Hancock, Charles Jones, and The George W. Strake, Jr. Foundation for their financial support and efforts to disseminate this work in philosophical reading. I thank my wife Lorraine, my daughter Korri, and my sons Paul and Peter for their patient support while I worked to complete the original monograph. Finally, I thank Kelly Fitzsimmons Burton, Ph.D., CEO and Founder of Public Philosophy Press for scanning and correcting the original text of *How to Read a Difficult Book*. Thanks also to Faith and Ethan Reece for helping to correct errors in the scanning process. They did an excellent job.

FOREWORD

No simple method exists to teach people how to read difficult books. Reading is a habit. We acquire habits by practice. For most of us, practice is difficult. For this reason alone, no simple way is likely to exist to teach us how to read difficult books. Generally, by difficult books we mean works that contain great truths, things that are usually hard for us to understand. For these reasons, I have written this work as a difficult book about how to read difficult books.

While this work is difficult, I have made every effort to simplify its contents. Primarily, I have written this work for classroom use, with a teacher's help. But I have also organized it for use in seminar discussions and personal study.

By dividing the book into sharply indicated, and usually short sections, and by providing Questions for Study and Discussion at the back of the book, I have sought to make this work easy for classroom and seminar use. If it is used in the classroom, I suggest that the class work with it in the following way: (1) Read a short selection, either an entire short section, or part of a longer section, for about five to ten minutes. (2) After reading the section, with the teacher acting only as a moderator to direct questions, student should discuss among themselves their opinions about the meaning of what they have just read. (3) After students have discussed their opinions about the selection they have just read, the classroom teacher should select some questions for them to discuss from the corresponding section of the Questions for Study and Discussion. The Questions do not necessarily directly relate to what the students have read. This lack of direct relation between a reading section and the Questions for Study and Discussion is intentional, not a mistake in the text. In most cases, the Questions deal with other issues related to learning and reading. I give my own answers to some of these Questions in different parts of the text. I provide these Questions to encourage students to think about and discuss problems as independent learners and a community of inquiry, not to have them accept my views as unquestionable truths. Their answers might be better than mine. (4) As much as possible, readers should hunt for definitions and examples in each selection they read. They should try to use these definitions and examples when they try to answer Questions. (5) As students read, teachers should check their eye movement, and call their attention back to the text if their minds tend to wander off. To assist in this effort, readers should avoid wearing objects that obscure the classroom teacher's vision of their eye movement, like hats and sunglasses. (6) Readers should follow the text with some sort of marker in hand, such as a pen or pencil. (7) As much as possible, readers should outline sections after they read them and should try to summarize what they have just read.

I wish all who read this book success in the pursuit of higher education. I hope they find this work useful in their quest.

Peter A. Redpath

INTRODUCTION

A. The State of Philosophical Reading: Yesterday and Today

More than fifty years ago, Mortimer J. Adler, current Chairman of the Board of Editors of the *Encyclopaedia Britannica*, and one of the most respected educators of the twentieth century, wrote his best-selling work, *How to Read a Book*. Within that best-seller, Adler made several startling statements. For example, he said that, after he had left Columbia University, he discovered he "could not read."[1] Dr. Adler did not mean that he could not sound out, or understand the meaning of, the words used by the author of a text. He meant that he did not possess the ability to read skillfully, to understand the meaning of a book as a whole and grasp how its component parts comprised its makeup.

He blamed his own poor reading ability on two main sources: (1) the curriculum of American schools which, he said, was "too crowded with other time-consuming things to permit enough attention to be given to the basic skills," and (2) that "most educators do not know how to teach the art of reading."[2] He added that a main reason most educators lack the know-how to teach the art of reading is that the skills needed to teach this art "have been almost lost."[3]

To support his claims, Adler referred to several major educational studies of the day. One was contained in an article written for *The Atlantic Monthly* by a Professor James Mursell from Columbia's Teacher's College entitled "The Defeat of the Schools," which, Mursell had said, was based upon "thousands of investigations" and "the consistent testimony of thirty years of enormously varied research in education." A large portion of that testimony reportedly came from a "recent survey of the schools of Pennsylvania carried on by the Carnegie Foundation." In reference to the mastery of the English language and of the ability to read, Mursell said:

> What about English? Here, too, there is a record failure and defeat. Do pupils in school learn to read their mother tongue effectively? Yes and no. Up to the fifth and sixth grade, reading, on the whole, is effectively taught and well learned. To that level, we find a steady and general improvement, but beyond it the curves flatten out to a dead level. This is not because a person arrives at his natural limit of efficiency when he reaches the sixth grade, for it has been shown again and again that with special tuition much older children, and also adults, can make enormous improvement. Nor does it mean that most sixth-graders read well enough for all practical purposes. A great many pupils do poorly in high school because of sheer ineptitude in getting meaning from the printed page. They can improve; but they don't.
>
> The average high—school graduate had done a great deal of reading, and if he goes on to college he will do a great deal more; but he is likely to be a poor and incompetent reader. (Note that this holds true of the *average* student, not a person who is a subject for special remedial treatment.) He can follow a simple piece of fiction and enjoy it. But put him up against a closely written exposition, a carefully and economically stated argument, or a passage requiring critical consideration, and he is at a loss. It has been shown, for instance, that the average high school student is amazingly inept at indicating the central thought of a passage, or the levels of emphasis and subordination in an argument or exposition. To all intents and purposes he remains a sixth grade reader till well along in college.[4]

Adler maintained that, even after graduating from a university, the reading ability of American students around 1940 had not progressed much beyond a sixth-grade level. He claimed that Mursell's evaluation of the condition of American literacy extended to post-university students throughout all the United States. To support this contention, Adler cited a New York State Board of Regents study of high school graduates that asserted that large numbers of them were "seriously deficient in the basic tools of learning" in such areas as the "ability to read" and to "understand straight-forward English."[5] He followed this up with results reported by a Professor Dietrich, from the Department of Education, at a four-day conference on reading held at the University of Chicago for teachers in 1939. Professor Dietrich's results were based upon "a test given at the University of Chicago to the best high school seniors who came there from all parts of the country to compete for scholarships." Reportedly, he told the thousand teachers assembled "that most of these very 'able' students could not understand what they read."[6]

When Adler made these statements, he was among the most highly educated college graduates and educators in the United States. Yet he reported that, when he had graduated college, he did not know how to read skillfully. And neither did most Americans, including his university teaching colleagues.

Adler's observations made over fifty years ago are worthy of reconsidering today for several reasons, one of which Adler gives:

> If one could elaborate all the essentials which a sound educational programme must consider, I should say that the techniques of communication, which make for literacy, are our first obligation, and more so in a democracy than in any other kind of society, because it depends on a literate electorate.[7]

In a democracy, the people rule. No political society can long flourish or survive when the hands of power are held by illiterate rulers. The existence of such a condition, especially in a democracy, is intolerable.

Another reason for reconsidering Adler's observations now is because of how timeless is his lament! Battalions of Americans today say the same things about high school and college students that Adler reported over fifty years ago. Today, just as in 1940, as Adler said:

> The complaints come from all sources. Business men, who certainly do not expect too much, protest the incompetence of the youngsters who come their way after school. Newspaper editorials by the score echo their protests and add a voice of their own, expressing the misery of the editor who has to blue-pencil the stuff university graduates pass across his desk.[8]

While Adler's observations are a sad indictment of the general incompetence of American educators, they should be a cause of hope for many American high school and college students who are constantly and continuously being criticized by many of these same educators for not being educationally motivated and for lacking educational skills. True, many American high school and college students are grossly illiterate. But, if such is the case, a main burden of responsibility for this state of affairs has to fall upon the shoulders of American educators, many of whom are also illiterate, and who are involved in attempting to communicate to their students a curriculum that students very often correctly recognize is filled with junk.

Contemporary students should not be disheartened by much of the criticism that currently comes their way. The same criticism has been coming the way of American students for most of this century. Students of this generation are no less lacking in natural ability than were students in previous generations in this century. If anything, they are simply a little more illiterate than some students of the past. And a main reason for this is that even less demands have been made of them to learn to read skillfully than were made of students of previous generations. So, they have a little more catching up to do. Still, they have a greater number of more powerful resources available to them today to make up for lost time in their reading development, including this book.

B. The Main Problem

I have written this book to help students learn how to read difficult books in a skillful way because I think this is the greatest obstacle to most students getting a higher education. Other problems exist in higher education today: open enrollment, decline of standards, mediocrity of curriculum, and so on. Despite what many educators might think, student motivation and ability to think logically and reason critically are not top on the list. In general, today's students are no less capable of thinking logically and of reasoning critically than they were in the last generation. Student ability and motivation are not the main educational problems today. To think that they are is to misconceive the main difficulty that we face in contemporary American higher education.

Somewhere, Etienne Gilson once remarked that most major philosophical problems arise from badly framed questions.[9] This is as true of educational problems as of any other philosophical problem. Failure precisely to identify and correctly to order the major problems facing higher education will delay their solution. The main problem we face in higher education today is general illiteracy, the general inability on the part of Americans to understand how to read skillfully, to extract meanings from the printed page, not the inability to think logically or critically, open enrollment, poor self-image, or discrimination.[10]

C. The Main Remedy

Such being the case, the main remedy for this problem lies in teaching high school and college students, and others, critical, or philosophical, reading, not critical thinking, or composition skills, unless, by these, we mean classical philosophical reasoning skills. This also means that while, in some cases, we might have to make sweeping changes in the content of curriculum in colleges and universities, in many cases we need pedagogical, not curriculum changes. Because high school and college students lack abstract reading skills, to attempt to improve their learning ability through a lecture, or curriculum changes, is largely useless. Instead, at least some high school and college classes (lower-level classes) need to be workshops in which we teach students to learn how to abstract the content of texts by reading portions of them from books in class, followed by teacher and student discussion of that material. One of these classes needs to examine the nature of learning, reading, a book, the liberal arts, classical philosophy, and philosophical reading of liberal arts texts.

This last point is crucial because the liberal arts and philosophy are language arts, essential skills of communication related to the way we transmit information through speech, primarily in connection with our eyes and ears, memory, imagination, intellect.

Among other things, the liberal arts and classical philosophy teach reading skills. Because we have lost our appreciation and understanding of the nature of these subjects, our culture is gradually becoming increasingly illiterate. The chief remedy to this problem is to regain an understanding of how to read a book as a liberal and philosophical artist.

If all we need to do to reform American higher education is to reestablish our understanding of how to read a book skillfully, perhaps we should simply read Adler's *How to Read a Book*. I heartily urge everyone to read this book. But I do not think Adler's book is enough to remedy this situation. If it were, since it was written over 50 years ago, why are Americans today generally no better readers than they were in 1940?

My answer is that, today, Dr. Adler's book is not enough. The audience for which he wrote was a general adult readership, not high school and college students. He did not design his book primarily for use in class as part of the course curriculum. And, even though the language he uses is simple enough in general, too often he employs terms and expressions, even in the most recent revised and updated version, that unnecessarily hinder the comprehension of today's average high school or college student. From a pedagogical standpoint, his text is unnecessarily difficult for classroom use.[11]

Adler's treatment of the liberal arts is also inadequate because he neglects to examine parts of the traditional liberal arts that would be most helpful for contemporary students to understand. Many of his insights about how to read are taken from the curriculum and methods of the later medieval schools and universities. Adler said that the lost arts of reading were: "the liberal arts which were once called grammar, logic, and rhetoric..., the arts of reading and writing, speaking and listening."[12]

Adler's understanding of the liberal arts is inaccurate. Therefore, his treatment of "the arts of reading and writing, speaking and listening" is inadequate. The traditional liberal arts were seven in number, not three. And, in some way, they are all related to the Western development of reading and writing, speaking and listening, and of higher education in general. These seven traditional liberal arts were grammar, rhetoric, logic, arithmetic, geometry, astronomy, and music. In Latin, the first three (grammar, rhetoric, and logic) were called the trivium (the three ways) and the last four were called the quadrivium (the four ways).

Even if Adler's identification of the liberal arts were accurate. his treatment of critical reading would still be inadequate. He misunderstands this type of skillful reading to involve simply engaging in a grammatical, logical, and rhetorical (or liberal arts) reading of a book. Critical reading involves more than this: reading a book artistically and philosophically. This is precisely why this sort of reading matured during the later Middle Ages within the context of medieval commentaries on philosophical writings of Aristotle.

Finally, Adler fails to make points and distinctions about the nature of learning, the nature and makeup of a book, and philosophical reading skill that are useful for beginning students of philosophical reading, be they high school or college students, or part of a more general readership. I make these points and distinctions in this text. While I have primarily designed this book for classroom use, as part of a high school or college curriculum, any adult with average reading ability can benefit from reading this work.

Chapter 1

LEARNING, TOOLS, BOOKS, AND PHILOSOPHICAL READING

A. Learning

To understand the nature of reading and of books, we need to understand, as Mortimer J. Adler has noted, that reading is a kind of learning.[1] At the very least, learning involves adding to our knowledge. So, reading, as a kind of learning, must help us add to our knowledge.

We add to our knowledge in several ways. As far back as Socrates, thinkers recognized that people could add to their knowledge with, or without, the help of teachers. Whichever approach we take to learning, we always engage in discovery.[2] We can learn by discovering things on our own, or we can learn with the help of independent discoverers, who can transmit their learning to others (teachers).

In either case, we can consider students to be discoverers. When we set out to learn things on our own, we are, in a way, students of nature ("nature" meaning ourselves and our surroundings). When we learn with the help of teachers, we are more than students of nature, because we are students of nature with the help of an individual, living part of nature, another human being.

This distinction between students of nature and more than students of nature (that is, students of nature with the help of other people) is crucial to recognize because it leads to a further distinction in learning, between learning with the help of classroom teachers or with the help of remote teachers. People who help us to learn are sometimes present and at hand. Sometimes they are remote from us in time and space, either because they are deceased, or because, while not dead, they are not present to us in space and or time.[3]

B. Tools

We can distinguish between classroom learning and remote learning because we can use specialized tools to learn. To understand how this occurs, we need to consider something about a tool's nature.

Tools are things that people, and other beings, put to use. Only God can work without tools. Tools receive, contain, hold, or transport, and extend action. For example, a phone, in a way, receives, contains, holds, transports, and extends the human voice, similar to the way a vegetable truck receives, contains, holds, transports, and extends a farmer's activity, or any truck receives, contains, transports, and extends cargo.

Tools are essential for performing any human action. For this reason, the ancient Greeks called human body parts "organs" (from the Greek word, organon, meaning a tool). Parts of the human body, such as the hand, foot, eye, ear, and mouth, receive, contain, transport, and extend human activity to another body or the action of another body to a human being.

Tools can be physical or non-physical, living or non-living, natural or artificial. For example, a rock can be a tool and so can an idea. A body part can be a tool, and so can a human faculty. We can use sight as a tool for remembering, and speech as a tool of the human mind to communicate ideas. An animal, such as a "beast of burden," like a mule or an ox, can be a tool. And so, can people, and not in the derogatory sense of being slaves or of being "used" by someone for morally questionable purposes. For example, a person who is paid a salary by a business is very much a business commodity and should no more be misused than should a machine. Any person performing a service acts the part of a living tool by receiving, containing, holding, transporting, and extending human actions. Hence, a diner who orders a hamburger in a restaurant is not personally cooking the hamburger but gets it by using another person's actions to receive, contain, hold, transport, and extend the directions of the diner.

By reducing time and space, tools receive, contain, extend, and transport, or hold, temporal and spatial actions. We always use tools in time and space. A tool's essential function in receiving, containing, holding, transporting, and extending action is to contract the time and space between individuals.[4] In saving time and space, human tools are labor-saving devices. They reduce the time and space we require to perform work. As labor-saving devices, tools reduce the exertion of human effort by eliminating obstacles to work performance. Hence, when we use tools rightly (which is the only way, precisely speaking, they are actually tools at all), tools promote human leisure.[5]

Strictly speaking, tools communicate knowledge and something good. All tools are helpful. And nothing can be helpful without, in some way, being good. A roof, for example, is helpful only to the extent that it is a good roof: insofar as it is complete as a roof, and, therefore, has no defects that would prevent it from keeping out hostile elements of weather while keeping in elements conducive to human safety.

Only some things can be tools. A thing becomes a tool only when it is used productively or helpfully for an agent. This requires that a tool transport skill a property of intelligence. If a refrigerator is not intelligently made or used, it will not be a good tool for containing, extending, and holding ice cream. Nor will a truck, or a hammer, which is not skillfully made or driven. All tools must transport human communication. Communication is transported intelligence.

Consider a simple tool sold in a grocery store: a fork or knife. The knife and fork communicate human intelligence (information) and skill, and so does the building considered in itself. The design of the knife and fork (or ice cream) and their packaging communicate to a shopper something about their use. If a manufacturer were unable so to communicate the use of the product to people skilled at its use, that person would soon be out of business. So, too, would the grocery store or restaurant owner whose building was not useful for its activity. It would not reflect the nature of the acts conducted within. And people would not patronize it.

Intelligent design of a tool always depends on at least five things: (1) the nature and abilities of the individual using the tool, (2) the work for which the tool will be put to use, (3) the tool's make-up, (4) how the tool will be used, and (5) the make-up, magnitude, and quality of the object to which the tool will be applied. The way we make a saw depends upon who will cut, what that person will cut, how that person will activate the tool, and the condition of the thing to be cut. So, we will not make a well-designed saw, for a professional carpenter, who will power the saw electrically to cut hard, thick wood, in the same way as we make a saw for a non-professional for general, hand-powered, use on soft, thin woods. We also manufacture trucks to carry items internally, externally, with hitches, under the frame, and so on, but only to the extent that these items are of a certain size and weight to be manageable by a particular driver. Tools have limits to their use. The material composition and design of tools reflect this limitation. For this reason, a person can often tell a lot about a tool and its use simply by looking at its make-up and design.

C. Books and Reading

Awareness of the above points about tools helps us to understand the nature and importance of books. Books are human tools. And all tools do useful things for us. They: (1) are essential for the performance of any human action, (2) receive, contain, hold, or transport, and extend human activity, (3) reduce the time and space that separate people from one another or from other things, (4) save on labor, (5) promote leisure, (6) receive, contain, hold, or transport, and extend human knowledge.

To understand books and why they are especially helpful to us, we have to recognize what sorts of tools they are. Like any tool, a book is only useful to a person who possesses the skill to put it to use. And not every book is designed to be put to use by everyone.

Principally and primarily, books are listening and hearing devices for transporting human knowledge in the form of trapped memory over time and space. Some readers might find it strange to *hear* books described as listening and hearing devices. But, in a way, this is most precisely what they are. We make books out of words. First and foremost, words are forms of speech.[6] Speech is a form of sound (a figured sound with length). And sound is transported, first and foremost, to human beings by listening tools. Hence, in a way, reading must be a kind of listening tool.

Consider writing. Writing is a tool of human activity by which we understand and transport words from writers to readers. Writers write for readers. No readers, no writers. Reading is a tool of human activity by which a reader receives and understands words transported from a writer. If no writers existed, no readers could exist.

Writing is a tool (in the form of a living, human activity and habit) for representing sound in the form of a figured line, called a letter or a word. Writing is a kind of engraving or painting that represents a sound through use of geometrical lines, angles, and curves. This means that, if human beings did not make sounds, they could never orally speak. Because we generally first tend to speak by using our mouths by making sounds, and because these sounds have uniform and regular dimensions to them (some are short, others long; some are high, others, low), we can represent these sounds through uniform and regular geometrical lines and figures, if and when people learn enough geometry to be able to engrave or to paint. In this way, we learn to write. Writing is a speaking tool, transferred through the use of engraved or painted, figured lines as tools, for receiving, containing, holding, transporting, and extending human speech. Similarly, reading is a hearing tool that enables us to hear, listen, and understand extended speech in the form of meaningful engraved or painted, figured and angled lines: words.

We do not hear the directly audible sound by this transferred form of listening any more than, by braille, we read the directly visible word. In braille, a blind person indirectly reads through the sense of touch. In reading, a person with normally healthy hearing listens indirectly through sight to meaningful words contained in the memory of a person not immediately present to us. Writing is a tool through which integratively we use human faculties (such as the mind, hands, memory, imagination, and eyes) to trap and wrap the spoken word within figured and angled, engraved or painted, lines. Writing transports these wrapped sounds to a listener, who, normally, through the use of similar faculties, but in a different way, abstractly unwraps and untraps these spoken words and further extracts from them the information that the words transport.

To understand this complex, human, abstracting activity called "reading," consider the state of human education prior to the development of books. Wherever this situation exists, one person alone arises to the state of chief educator within a culture: a person with an exceptionally good memory who can preserve a people's language. This happens because no human culture exists where no skill exists. Human culture is more than an association of people: an association of people possessed of skill, able to transmit this skill from one generation to the next. Without language arts, such transmission is humanly impossible. Human beings communicate knowledge to one another through physical signs, language arts. Where people have no writing skills, the culture becomes most dependent upon the person with a good memory who is well versed in language (an epic poet) to transmit its memory about its skills and their importance from one generation to the next.

When the tools for transmitting human memory through speech evolve to use of the written word, then the central importance of an epic poet as educator declines. This becomes a less attractive line of work for the economically concerned person to enter than the profession of a scribe. And the scribe's line of work becomes crucial to education until the mechanized printed book comes along.[7]

Whether a book is produced manually, through a scribe's work, mechanically through a press, or electronically through a word processor, the product is the same: a tool for receiving, containing, holding, transporting, and extending human memory in the form of speech across expanses of time and space. In so doing, a book is one of the most crucial of all cultural tools. It enables us to preserve and transport valuable information across generations. It allows people in the present to listen to and learn from the words of past great discoverers, as students from teachers. Not to understand this quality of books is a great and tragic loss for anyone, especially for anyone who wants to learn.

Three more points are crucial to appreciate more completely the nature of a book as a tool of human learning.

One is that the memory that books trap and convey is always in the form of some main conversation.[8] To be able to write in an intelligible way, an author must consider how the written word will sound to a reader. Every author must read the work being written as a member of a potential audience.

The second point is that human knowledge is an activity of a living, physical being. As such, it is subject to the same limiting spatial and temporal conditions that all physical things suffer. All physical actions have a temporal and spatial beginning, middle, and end. Human knowledge, in the form of a recollected conversation, is no exception. Consequently, all books have a beginning, middle, and end.

The third point is that all conversations concern something specific and individual. People do not discuss something like baseball in general, but some individual team or player, at a specific time, place, and so on.

These three points are crucial to recognize because, to be able to listen to and hear what an author says in a book, we must listen in much the same way as we listen to a verbal conversation. Verbal conversations always concern some general and particular topic. If we want to join in a conversation with others, we can only do so productively if we know something about the general and particular topic. Since conversations have a beginning, middle, and an end, and sometimes cover a wide variety of specific topics always related to some general topic, to follow the conversation in detail, we also need to know how the conversation began and how it developed up to the point at which the listener entered upon the scene. Finally, points exist at which various sub-topics break off in a conversation and others begin. To follow a conversation, we need to know when these sub-topics switch.

I point out these things in the above paragraph because, often, when we start to read a book, we pay no attention at the beginning to the book's main, or most general, topic. Unless we know this, we cannot know what the conversation of the book is all about. We necessarily get lost. Not because we lack intelligence. But because we fail to practice the art of reading. Secondly, sometimes, even though we might know what a book generally is about, we decide to stop reading at a point in the conversation that is right in the middle of one topic. Then we attempt to resume reading without attempting to recall what was the topic under discussion when we left off. To proceed in this fashion makes no more sense than to attempt to do a series of fifty math problems in which, to solve each successive problem, we must first solve the one before. If we decide to stop doing a problem right in the middle, and then to return to solving the series without considering the first part of the math problem where we left off, we have to get lost, no matter how intelligent we might otherwise be. And the rest of the series of problems will, likewise, become unintelligible to us.

This problem is not a lack of mathematical reasoning skills, but of poor reading habits. The way to resolve such a problem is through a course on critical listening, observing, and reading, not a course on critical thinking.

D. Powerful and Critical Reading and Critical Thinking

The last point I made in the preceding paragraph is crucial because it indicates that we cannot acquire critical thinking skills without developing critical and powerful reading skills. Critical thinking presupposes critical and powerful reading. We do not need to think critically when the things we consider are easy to understand. We need critical thinking when we attempt to understand things that are above our heads, things that we can generally grasp only through hard work and teaching assistance. Such thinking demands that we possess a critically trained and powerful memory, because thinking presupposes the possession and use of memory. Critical thinking, therefore, must presume that we possess a critically-trained memory. Human memory, however, only becomes activated through stimulation by sense images. Without a critically-trained imagination, we cannot become critically-trained thinkers. To possess a critically-trained imagination, we must have a rich, varied, flexible, powerful imagination, the kind that we can only acquire through numerous and varied sense experiences and memories. We can only develop such experiences and memories through rich, varied, flexible, and powerful language skills in all the general areas of human knowing, abilities that are out of reach of the ordinary individuals working without the aid of great teachers.

In short, to become powerful, critical thinkers, we must first become critical and powerful observers, listeners, speakers, imaginers, and recollectors. None of this is possible without the help of great teachers and hard work. To come into direct contact with such teachers in the numbers necessary to maximize the ability to achieve the highest levels of education is a practical impossibility for anyone today. Without help from critical and powerful listening tools and skills provided by critical and powerful reading, virtually no human being can possess the linguistic skills necessary to acquire the developed imaginations and memories required to become a critical and powerful thinker.

Chapter 2

THE SKILL OF PHILOSOPHICAL READING

A. Three Purposes of Learning, Listening, and Reading

Since reading is a transferred way of listening and hearing, to learn to read skillfully we must listen and hear skillfully. We do so by attending directly to the written, not the spoken, word. Reading is more than an act of transferred visual listening and hearing: a way of listening to learn something. This means that, since learning has different purposes, different kinds of listening exist. And, because different kinds of listening exist, different kinds of reading exist.

Mortimer J. Adler has aid, most generally, that learning has three different purposes: (1) enjoyment, (2) information, and (3) enlightenment.

When we seek to increase knowledge by personal discovery or with the help of a teacher, we are motivated to do so by at least one, two, or three goals: (1) to enjoy something, (2) to enjoy something or increase personal information, (3) to enjoy something, or increase our information or enlightenment.[1]

Sometimes we want to increase our knowledge for personal amusement. At other times, we want to increase our knowledge to acquire some information that is not difficult to understand. At other times, we want to learn something to get some information that is "over our heads," not easy for us to understand, but desired nonetheless.[2]

Whenever we seek to learn, to some extent, we always seek enjoyment and addition of information. In a way, whenever we learn we always increase of understanding, if only of our own ignorance. One of these factors always predominates as our main motive for learning. Hence, we can divide learning, listening, and reading into three kinds: for (1) enjoyment, (2) information, and (3) enlightenment.

B. Learning for Enlightenment, Listening, and Liberal Arts

Strictly speaking, we need no special skill to read for enjoyment and amusement. Every skill involves being able to do something difficult and exceptional. All reading requires some skill, that, by its nature as a skill, is critical and powerful. But any person who has acquired an average reading ability can read for enjoyment and information. Such is not the case when we read for enlightenment. Here, we try to discover something we cannot easily discover on our own, using, at least, only nature as a teacher. In this situation, we must usually learn with the additional assistance of another person. If that person is a classroom teacher, or a person ready at hand, then, under normal circumstances, we can be helped to learn with that person's assistance by listening to the directions that person directly gives.

In this situation, we must exert more intense and abstract listening than we use to apprehend something amusing or to gain some familiar information. When we learn from remote teachers through use of books, we cannot read books for enlightenment in the same way that we read books for amusement or for familiar information. The magnitude of difficulty of the material that we seek to understand demands a greater magnitude of abstract effort and power to grasp. This situation requires is higher level reading skill, reading as a liberal art.

C. The Nature of a Skill

To understand what reading as a liberal art involves, we must first understand what is an art or skill. To do this, in turn, we need to consider how we acquire arts or skills: by practice. We lose them through debility, or forgetting how to do something. Possession of a memory makes acquisition and loss of arts and skills possible. Only a living being possessed of a memory can practice and forget (because practice requires repetition).[3]

The human intellect applies (and, so, *uses*) the memory to a particular human faculty to imbed that faculty with memory and enable it to perform its natural organic act with greater precision and strength. Human faculties such as eyes and ears, imagination, and intellect, perform specific actions in conjunction with natural organic functions. Our organs are not born maturely developed. They have to grow to maturity through the exercise of living action, such as seeing and hearing. Because children perform human acts through immaturely-developed organs, they cannot, at first, do these acts with securely-possessed precision. They bring these organic acts to mature and precise exercise by directing their operation through the human memory.

Such acts are acts of sense knowing. But they are also acts of sense learning. The act of learning involves more than adding to our knowledge. For this reason, people can have a lot of experience of something and still not have learned anything about it. Learning involves an ability to identify a thing through some abstract and precise grasp of the different parts that comprise its make-up. To learn involves coming to know something by becoming *abstractly familiar* with the parts that make it to be some one thing, and not another. Becoming abstractly familiar with something involves apprehending a thing with a lot of memory. As a result, people with skill tend to be familiar with the subject of their skill.

Often, we refer to this imbedded memory in a human faculty, the source of human skill, as a habit. Hence, learning, as a skill or an art, is a habit.

D. The Nature of Learning and Reading as Liberal Arts

Childhood and early adolescent learning primarily involves our intellects working to gain precise control over our external and internal sense faculties by habituating these faculties under the intellect's direction of sense memory and imagination. As the sense faculties mature, through use of memory, our intellects exercise increasing control over them. Central to this process is the flexibility of our imaginations to take direction from our memories. Our imaginations are flexible to the extent that they are fertile. And, just as the external sense faculties know to the extent that they can extract sensible content from their contact with sensible things, so our imaginations begin their activities to the extent that we can unwrap, or abstract, imaginable content given to the external senses in trapped form in acts of external sensation, such as seeing and hearing.

At first, the images that our imaginations extract from external acts of sensing are crude constructions. Hence, when young children first attempt to imagine what they have just seen or heard, they have difficulty forming distinct images of these external sense events. The imagination has not been habituated to direct its activities with abstract precision through the reasoned application of the human memory to the exercise of its own specific activity. As our images of acts of seeing, hearing, touching, and other external sense activities become more abstractly precise, we become more capable of representing imaginable content in a more refined, uniform, and contracted way. We start to represent images in a standardized way by engraved or figured, angled lines, in pictures. And our minds give birth to the spoken and written word, and rudimentary acts of reading.[4] After this, through further contraction, uniformity, and refinement of sensible images, we elevate human language to a level of imaginative abstraction in which we start to use a phonetic alphabet to represent imaginative content to our memories and intellects.

Since use of memory and emotions gradually imbeds the different sense and intellectual faculties with intellectual volitional direction, eventually our intellects and wills can imbed these faculties with habits. Through linguistic development our imaginative content gains uniformity and simplicity. This enables us to prepare the human memory eventually to serve the human intellect in such a way as to raise intellectual activity to a level of highest human learning. This requires refined and uniform content in the human imagination and mnemonic placement and positioning of this content in temporal and spatial order. As our intellects start habitually to apprehend ideas, under mnemonic direction, we start to elevate human language to the level of a tool that can provide our imaginations with the kind of uniform, regular, and flexible images that we need for our intellects to do scientific work.

Recall that we call the "liberal arts" the ancient Greeks first called "music." Reportedly, music was produced by the daughters of Zeus and Memory, the Muses. These were fine arts, habituating the imagination and memory to produce specifically human activities under direction of general rules inspired supposedly by the gods or the natural inspiration of the human intellect.[5] As such, the liberal arts were and are primarily language, not servile, arts. As language arts, they require some association with arts of measurement (what Medieval thinkers called the quadrivium). The writer, reader, speaker, and listener have to have a sense of order, due proportion, position, placement, geometrical line, surface, length, height, depth, breadth and so on just to transform a sound into a spoken letter or written word, or to transform an image as a picture or hieroglyph into the refined figured, angular, line engraving or drawing of the phonetic letter.

Such arts are liberal because they free our minds by giving us essential tools to do intellectual natural work in a more precise and exact, or critical and powerful way. The human intellect becomes active only when it is presented with some sort of imaginable content. None of us can comprehend anything intellectually unless we can first *imagine it in the right way*. For our intellects to be able to conceptualize about a rich and wide variety of things in uniform and regular ways, something that scientific thought demands, we must first be capable of imagining things in a richly, uniformly, and regularly. Sophisticated scientific work demands sophisticated language skills because sophisticated language skills give us rich, varied, uniform, and regular ways to imagine things. For this reason, premature specialization kills the scientific intellect. It stunts free play of the human imagination upon which depend imaginative refinement and intellectual maturity in directing scientific activity.

Achieving critical reading and human science is *hard work*, demanding a totally different way of using human memory than commonly happens in primary and secondary education. In scientific work, our memories help elevate our intellects to an entirely new, habitual, abstract, and specialized way of abstracting and organizing ideas and judgments. To be able to help our intellects perform this lofty work, we need highly sophisticated and powerful language skills, that we can only acquire by using highly-trained, powerful, and abstractive listening skills reflecting upon the writing of great discoverers.

The language problem related to science is evident. Most great discoverers are not ready at hand to help teach people in the classroom. Most are remote from us in time and space. Yet only through contact with them, by abstractly listening to their words, can we raise the content of our imaginations to a level that the ongoing work of human science demands. People who desire to achieve higher learning must read the works of great teachers or great discoverers, most of whom are few in number, dead, or geographically or temporally absent. This means that to be *higher educated, it is not as important to be widely read as it is to be wisely read.*[6] From the standpoint of achieving higher education, not all books are of equal value. From this standpoint, a little bit of reading of a few great books for understanding is worth much more than extensive amounts of reading of many books for simply amusement or information.[7]

Chapter 3

GENERAL TYPES OF BOOKS AND KINDS OF TEACHING

A. General Types of Books

On the basis of the distinction between the two different kinds of learning by discovery, we can, in general, distinguish between two major types of books according to their importance: (1) original works written by great discoverers and (2) secondary sources (works of less important discoverers, written for general enjoyment or amusement, and informational works that are commentaries or aids to understanding the works written by great discoverers, such as periodical journals, encyclopedias, and other kinds of reference works). Today, we often call the first type of work "great books," and the second "secondary sources."[1]

This distinction is crucial in relation to understanding general approaches that we have to take to comprehend a book's contents and the general division of reading material that libraries make. Like books, colleges, universities, and other learning institutions, libraries are tools for receiving, containing, holding, transporting, and extending human learning through preservation of (1) the knowledge of great discoverers over generations, and (2) the enabling means intellectually to unwrap, un-trap, and unravel the words and meanings contained in the major works of great discoverers. The way we divide libraries and universities reflects the kinds of works that, people of different cultures consider important to preserve and pass on from generation to generation.

Great books are important works written by major discoverers. These books are great precisely because they involve reports of great discoveries. For this reason, successive generations try to preserve reports of these discoveries. That we exert tremendous effort to preserve these works indicates their importance and the exceptional status of the people who wrote them.

Regarding the fact that great works are important discoveries made by great discoverers, Mortimer J. Adler observes that great universities are institutions at which great teachers teach. If such be the case, then the faculty of the greatest university consists of thinkers such as Socrates, Plato, Aristotle, Archimedes, Euclid, St. Augustine, St. Thomas Aquinas, Galileo, Leonardo da Vinci, Dante, Petrarch, Erasmus, Kepler, Newton, Shakespeare, Bacon, Descartes, Locke, Berkeley, Hume, Hobbes, Adam Smith, Kant, Spinoza, Hegel, Wordsworth, Shelly, Boyle, Dalton, Lavoisier, Pasteur, Faraday, Planck, Einstein, and so on. As Adler says:

> Would anyone want to go to any other university, if he could get into this one? There need be no limit on numbers. The price of admission—the only entrance requirement—is the ability and willingness to read. The school exists for everybody who is willing and able to learn from first-rate teachers, though they be dead in the sense of not jolting us out of our lethargy by their living presence. They are not dead in any other sense. If the contemporary world dismisses them as dead, then, as a well-known writer recently said, we are repeating the folly of the ancient Athenians who supposed that Socrates died when he drank the hemlock.[2]

B. General Kinds of Teaching

The general distinction between two different kinds of learning, and the distinction between two different kinds of books, leads to a third helpful distinction, between different kinds of classroom teaching. Adler rightly asserts that teachers are the "intellectual betters" of students. We only learn from our intellectual superiors, not our intellectual equals. The greatest discoverers are intellectually superior to all other discoverers. Hence, a person who transmits and comments upon the works of major thinkers in a classroom (the person we most often call a "teacher") is not our primary teacher. As Adler puts it, this person is simply a better student.[3] Hence, this person:

> should not masquerade as one who knows and can teach by virtue of his original discoveries, if he is only one who has learned through being taught. The primary sources of his knowledge should be the primary sources of learning for his students, and such a teacher functions honestly only if he does not aggrandize himself by coming between the great books and their young readers.[4]

If we accept Adler's observations about education as "the elevation of a mind by its betters,"[5] we can easily recognize that three kinds of teachers can exist: (1) originators of important discoveries, (2) facilitators of major discoveries, (3) mediators between students and great teachers of the past or present. Most classroom teachers do not fall into the first or second class of teachers. They are not original discoverers of great things. And they do not facilitate major discoveries, unless they are original discoverers or mediators of original discoveries by others. The most proper function teachers play in the classroom is reading supervisors. The main role of classroom teachers is to put students into first-hand communication with a great teacher by training them how to read that teacher's books, how to listen to and understand (hear) the words of that person as they were originally communicated, not to lecture to students about what a great teacher has told them about that teacher's own discoveries.[6]

Today, the most common forms of high school and college teaching range between (1) lecturing and (2) seminar discussions. In light of the primary role of the classroom teacher, at least on the level of introductory classes, both these teaching methods are wrong. The lecture causes a classroom teacher to masquerade as an original discoverer. This deprives us of first-hand contact with the major teachers of higher learning. The second method might put us into first-hand contact with such primary teachers, but it does so in the condition of untrained listeners. It deprives us of the necessary abstractive reading skills for extracting the meaning of the words to which we listen.

The most appropriate method for classroom instruction on the introductory high school or college level combines textual commentary and seminar discussion. It requires that we do supervised reading in class under the direction of someone trained to read a text abstractively, followed by a seminar discussion of question and answer during which any confusions we have can be aired and, hopefully, resolved.

Chapter 4

PHILOSOPHICAL READING AND DEFINITIONS

A. Philosophical Reading as a Liberal Art

Before I consider the most general division of books into their various kinds on the basis of their subjects, I need to make some points about the liberal art of reading as a learning tool. The art, or skill, of learning from others involves practice. We have to use our memories and imaginations, be able to listen to what a text says, know in a specific way.

All human knowing involves apprehending a whole by means of its parts. We cannot understand anything without thinking about it as a whole made up of parts. For example, if something had no parts (for instance, a pure spirit, like God, or something totally infinite) we could not know it, unless we conceived it in reference to something made up of parts. To test the truth of this claim, attempt to think of anything that is not, in some way, a whole, or if a whole, can be identified without reference to its parts. For example, if we think about a natural object, such as a rock or a dog, and attempt to identify each, in the case of a rock, we have to refer to some non-living body. Non-living and body are parts that compose the idea "rock" in much the same way that "living, sentient, body" compose the idea animal. Parts that comprise the idea of a thing are the means through which we come to know a thing. They constitute the thing's definition.

Parts that make up the whole idea of a thing are also the means through which we learn from one another. Learning from each other involves giving explanations to one another. And all explanations involve reasoning through definitions.

Definitions are tools of general identification, intellectual tools that we use to identify things in an assembly-line fashion so that we can cluster several individuals together in a kind of bunch, and know (or identify) them all together, in the same act. As such, definitions are intellectual labor-saving devices. They save us time and effort. For example, we can much more easily count by tens, and, twenties, and so on, than by ones.

Learning through use of an explanation, therefore, involves learning by applying definitions to individual examples, increasing our knowledge through collective identification of individual things.

I make this point because using books to learn always demands learning through use of explanation, an attempt to communicate ideas through word use. By listening to another person's words, we attempt to grasp that person's ideas. We can only grasp ideas by uniting their parts into a whole. We can only communicate ideas by wrapping them and trapping them in words, or other physical symbols, that serve as instances, examples of ideas. Also, we can only understand ideas by some reference to images. And we can only comprehend images through reference to some sensible object that we imagine. Hence, we can explain no idea without reference to an example.

Once we understand that all books are composed of conversations and explanations, we possess the essential tool for understanding how to read all books, even the most difficult. Since all books are made up of explanations, all books are made up of definitions.

This means that reading, especially higher level, or powerful and critical reading, must always involve a hunt for and an ability to abstract, or extract, (1) definitions and (2) the way that definitions organize the topics of conversation that comprise a book. Books are tools for receiving, containing, holding, extending, and transmitting knowledge through words formed into definitions within the context of conversations.

The whole act of reading, therefore, essentially involves understanding what a writer says by philosophically unpacking the meaning of the words that compose the book. To do this, we have to find and abstract the definitions that make the book intelligible as a whole.

B. Philosophical Reading and the Most General Kinds of Books

Knowing that powerful and critical reading principally and primarily involves a hunt for definitions gives us other essential pieces of the puzzle for understanding how to read any book: what kind of knowledge the writing transports, the subject of the book, and the general context of conversation that contain the definitions.

Knowing these things is crucial because the subject of the book, its main topic of conversation, determines the type of definitions that constitute its make-up. Not understanding the subject matter of a book dooms us to misunderstand its definitions.

To make my point clearer, let us divide all books into five general types of subjects: (1) books principally about theoretical matters of fact, (2) books principally about practical matters of fact, (3) books principally about mathematical measurement, (4) books principally about imaginable experiences, and (5) books principally involving mixed matters.[1]

On the basis of this division, in an outline, we can identify the types of books we generally read in high school and college, and most demand the skill of philosophical reading to master as:

A. Principally About Theoretical Matters of Fact
(1) Theology
(2) Philosophy
(3) Social Science
    a. History
    b. Psychology
    c. Sociology

      d. Anthropology

B. Principally About Mathematical Measurement
(1) Mathematics
(2) Physical Science
      a. Physics
      b. Chemistry
      c. Astronomy
      d. Biology

C. Principally About Practical Matters of Fact
(1) Computer Science
(2) Speech Communication
(3) Ethics
(4) Political Science
(5) Language

D. Principally About Matters of Imaginable Experiences
(1) Fictional Literature
(2) Poetry
(3) Painting and Sculpture
(4) Music
(5) Theater

    This division helps us because the context of any book is always something's existence, usually in time and place. All finite things exist inside or outside the physical world. If in the physical world, inside or outside human faculties and organs in the past, present, or future, or in times and places that are, were, will be, could be, should be, would be, or might be.

    I point these things out because human beings can know things in some most general ways, and none of us can know or think about all things in the same most general ways. We can think about some things in only a couple of general ways. We can think about others in many general ways. The people involved and the things and the contexts in which we consider things determine the way we generally think about things.

    We can never know or think about some things practically. Practical knowledge demands knowing or thinking about how to do or to make something. For many reasons, none of us can, in principle or actuality, know or think about how to do or to make many things. For example, we cannot, in principle, practically think about creating a world out of nothing because this requires infinite power, which no human being possesses. Hence, knowing how to create is not a practical possibility of human knowledge or thought, even in principle.

Similarly, at certain times and places, none of us can think practically about doing something that, at other times and places, becomes a practical possibility. For example, at present, practically thinking about flying to certain galaxies in a space ship tomorrow. While such a practical trip might be practically thinkable in the future, currently it is a practical, and actual, impossibility.

Knowing and thinking about things practically, then, involves knowing and thinking about things we can cause to be in the possible past, present, and future. This is not necessarily the case when we think about things theoretically or when we think about imaginable experiences. We can think about imaginable experiences practically, but we do not have to. And we can think about imaginable experiences as past, present, or future; about what could be, should be, would be, or might be.

Furthermore, all books must involve imaginable experiences because every book's author must imagine vocal sounds (words) as linear and curved figures (written sounds) in order to write a book. In this sense, every book is an imaginative creation. Moreover, we cannot think about historical matters in all these same ways. To think about events as historical, we have to imagine them as past. Since, strictly speaking, the past no longer exists, we cannot think of historical events practically, except as objects of the human imagination and memory. History studies the abstractly considered, or reconstructed, and imagined past to apprehend how, in the past, some whole event was made up of specific parts. As such, history is a reconstruction of imaginable experiences of what could have been. Since historical events have been, evidently they could be. For, if the events could not be, they could not have been.

While we tend to identify most professional philosophical work as theoretical thinking, philosophers are not limited to thinking about things theoretically, or at any one time or place.

Strictly speaking, ethics and politics are practical, not theoretical, philosophical disciplines. Ethics, for example, always studies human choice in relation to some aspect of futurity and human possibility, always considering what we have done, are doing, or will do as a choice that has or had a future and could have been done otherwise. Hence, in ethics, we might say that we should or should not do or have done an action because our choice had a different future possibility before we chose the action. Similarly, political philosophers might consider the past or the future, but, strictly speaking, as practical philosophers, they always do so with a view to future human possibilities, to learn from the past and the present and be prepared for the future.

Because most general and abstract ways exist by which we can know and think about things, and because we make books out of human knowledge, we can make most general and abstract divisions of books. Ignorance of this and failure to consider it when we begin to read something are obstacles to achieving a proper understanding of what an author has written.

Moreover, when we think about things theoretically, or speculatively, we need to recognize that we are thinking about something having some existence (real or otherwise) in the present. And, since all our knowledge involves apprehending wholes in terms of their parts, theoretical or speculative thinking involves knowing or thinking about things as if they were complete wholes made up of parts and were being resolved or divided into their component parts. Theoretical or speculative knowing is not a type of knowing by "guessing," which is what many people often mean when they use these words today. They are ways of knowing achieved by "viewing" or "looking at" a whole as made up of parts, or at parts as arranged in such a way as to make up a whole. Hence, when I say that I know Socrates speculatively or theoretically I might say that I know him to be a rational animal because these are the parts that make up his whole definition. To know theoretically or speculatively is to know some already existing whole through its constituent parts.

When we know something practically, we do not apprehend a whole in the same way, because the whole being known does not as yet exist. It only exists when we produce it through the act of "know how." Knowing things practically, therefore, does not involve viewing or looking at a whole through its constituent parts, but of causing parts to constitute a whole. As a result, practical thinking always involves thinking about parts and wholes as means to ends, the ends always being more general than, and achieved through, the means. A crucial point to note because whenever we apprehend things as wholes through their parts we grasp things through their definitions. This means that practical definitions always take on a specific formulation that prevents us from expressing them in simple declarative sentences. Practical definition involves organizing parts to constitute a whole, not observing or viewing the way a whole is made up of parts.

Matters of mathematical measurement, also, involve things that we can consider in several ways, theoretically, practically, imaginably, as past, present, future, and so on. Yet, whenever we measure, we apply a one to a many as a part to a whole. I will examine how this takes place in greater detail when I consider more specifically how to read works about matters of measurement.

Chapter 5

THREE RULES FOR "PHILOSOPHICALLY READING" ANY BOOK

A. Three Rules

Mortimer J. Adler has rightly noted that to read a difficult book we have to determine its nature and our motives for reading it. Is the book an original work written by an original discoverer, or a secondary source? Are we reading it for pleasure or amusement, information or enlightenment? Are we reading it primarily for theoretical or practical purposes? Is the content solely or primarily theoretical or practical information, about measurement, or about imaginable experiences?

These points are crucial to consider because books are tools. As tools, they are human artifacts. As artifacts, we determine their definition artificially, by how they are skillfully designed and used. While an author might have primarily written a book as a theoretical work, nothing prevents us from reading it for practical purposes. Similarly, nothing prevents us from reading for theoretical reasons works that authors primarily intended to be practical. Or from reading for enlightenment works written by authors primarily to amuse.

Once we determine what and why we are reading something, in the case of difficult books, the following procedure is helpful. First, always read with a pen, pencil, or some sort of marker, in hand, or with Post-its if reading a library book.

Second, have close at hand a notebook, typewriter, or word processor, with paper, or page orientation, wide enough to make a horizontal or landscape outline of the book's contents.

Third, as you begin to outline the book, read the book at least three times, becoming progressively more specific about the work's contents. Start by reading the book in a most general way (a general reading, to locate definitions and examples, not to understand precise details). Then in a less general way (a specific reading, to identify arguments). And, finally, in an individual way (a most precise reading, to understand precise details).[1]

B. Why Read with a Marking Device in Hand?

People who do not habitually mark up a book while reading might wonder why some people write in books. Many reasons might exist for this practice. One is that, by writing in a book, we can more easily retrieve information. Another is that, when we mark up a book, we start to engage the author in conversation in a more explicit and intense fashion. Philosophical reading involves intense and highly abstract listening. It demands that we listen and converse intensely with an author. A book's author is usually not immediately present in time and space to the reader. Hence, a reader has a problem engaging an author in conversation at all, especially intensely.

Given the restrictions on our ability to speak directly to an author, writing is the closest way readers can generally engage remote speakers in conversation. And, usually, the author cannot answer us. The conversation we have with the author generally takes place during the act of reading, not in the future, even if this is possible. Consequently, to compensate for our inability to engage the author in direct correspondence about the author's work, critical readers write in books. By so doing, we start to express our opinions about what an author says in one or another part of a text, and, at times, react to the author's views with our own. For example, often when I read a work, I write things in the margin, such as "Beautiful! See, page so and so below." Or, "Bah! You have got to be kidding me." Or "Aristotle disagrees." And so on. Furthermore, at times, I might revise a previous opinion and remark, "OK, now I see. See page so and so above."

Reading in this way makes the book take the form of a written conversation between a student and teacher and of a diary of our mental evolution. In this way, a book becomes a record for future reference about what we were thinking about a certain matter at a certain time. Such marks can become invaluable research tools for determining the way we arrived, step by step, at the views that we developed and the extent an author influenced our understanding in general and at specific times of our lives.

C. A Detailed Look at Rule Three: Progressive Reading of a Book

Regarding rule three, a most general reading of a difficult book is like separating the pieces of a complex puzzle before putting them together. Every book is made up of topics of conversation that an author arranges in an order of explicit or implicit definitions, examples, and arguments in relation to a most general, or main, topic. This topic determines the order or organization of all the other sub-topics, definitions, examples, and arguments. To read a book philosophically, we must first, in general, find out what it is about, just as when we first enter into a conversation we must first know in general what it is about before we can speak to the specific details. As readers, we first start to do this by paying attention to the book's title because the title generally reflects the book's most general topic of conversation, the topic to which, in some way, all the other sub-topics of conversation, definitions, examples, and arguments relate.

After we make note of the book's title, we should then survey the jacket for information about the author, take a look at the copyright page, the date of publication, the edition, table of contents, chapter headings and subheadings, glossary (if one exists), and index (again, if one exists). This information often gives us knowledge useful to understanding an author's intention, which often helps us unravel difficult textual passages. For example, by reading a book's jacket, we can get valuable biographical information about the author. This can help us grasp why or how the author tends to think about an issue. Similarly, by taking a look at the index, we can get some familiarity with the thinkers who might have influenced an author's opinion. By taking a look at the glossary, we become familiar with the author's technical vocabulary and definitions out of which the arguments that make up a difficult book are constituted. By surveying the copyright page, date of publication, and edition, we can get valuable information about the evolution of an author's thinking about a specific topic. And, having this information, we can read earlier and later versions of a work, and can note differences that have influenced changes in an author's views on different matters. Finally, by viewing the chapter headings and subheadings in relation to the title, we can get a general familiarity with a work that helps us to understand the organization of an author's arguments.

The table of contents helps us because its list of chapter headings gives us a general familiarity with a book's sub-topics of conversation. These act as parts of the book's entire conversation, and, according to their order of appearance, so to speak, *make up* the book. Hence, by doing a general reading of a book, the first thing we should do after gathering the necessary tools for recording the work's general contents and surveying its general structure is to start a numbered outline of the chapter headings, horizontally, if possible (so more material can fit across the page), in a notebook, or on a typed sheet of paper. This means that, on page one of our outline, in numerical order, matching the order of appearance in the text, we should write or type the book's title (and subtitle, if one exists) and the book's topics as they appear in the table of contents.

Next, we should turn to the page numbers that mark off the chapter headings, identify and copy into our outline (in the appropriate order of appearance under the appropriate chapters) whatever subheadings the author might have included.

After we do all these things, we have completed the book's general reading. And we are ready to start the next stage of philosophical reading: the specific reading.

D. Specific Reading of a Book

After we finish the general reading of a book, we have to grasp the order of appearance of the more specific details of topics or *contents* that compose a book. In this type of reading, we try to identify more precise, but not minute, details of conversation and their order of appearance in the text. To do these things, we must, first, note whether the book contains any characters or special temporal and spatial settings of the conversations. If so, we must put these in their appropriate places in our outline, according to their order of appearance within the text. For example, which character in which topic, or conversation, comes in first, second, and so on. If book has characters, we have to pay attention to what the characters do when they first enter the work. And we must pay special attention to what had happened in the story just before and after the character entered, because the character might introduce something into the story, such as a special question or problem.

Plato's masterpiece, the *Republic*, gives us a good example of why we need to pay attention to characters against the background of setting. Plato intends this work mainly as a philosophical book. As such, he mainly composes it of questions, problems, and arguments for rational consideration, not mystical contemplation. The Republic is also a dramatic work in which characters introduce the questions and problems. These characters appear in a temporal and spatial order. Hence, at the start of the *Republic*, Socrates has just finished making a sacrifice to the goddess Bendis at a festival at a port town, the Peiraeus, not far from Athens. Socrates says he had gone to the Peiraeus with Plato's brother Glaucon to make this offering to the goddess in whose honor the festival was being held. After fulfilling his religious duties, Socrates and Glaucon were about to leave for home. Polemarchos, son of an elderly and long-time local friend of Socrates, Cephalos, saw them about to leave, and sent his servant to catch them. Because Polemarchos is Cephalos's son and friend, when he hears that Socrates is about to depart, Polemarchos uses some strong-arm persuasion to get Socrates to stay, return to his house, and engage his father and some other people in conversation. When Socrates gets to the house, Cephalos, an elderly gentleman, is wearing a garland on his head because he has just made a sacrifice in his garden.

The main theme of the *Republic* is not, as we might suspect from the title, about making a city. Its primary concern is with the nature of justice and with attempting to show that the just person's, and city's, life is more powerful and happier that unjust one's. To get his readers to start reflecting upon this topic and move their minds through recollection from vague images to a refined concept of justice, Plato starts his dialogue by introducing two apparently just and wise people, Socrates and Cephalos, engaged in two apparently just acts (paying debts to the goddess). Then he has Socrates and the elder Cephalos talk about the relationship of old age to happiness by having Socrates ask the old man whether he thinks old age is a difficult time of life or not. As a great teacher and philosopher, Plato does this because he knows that, in some way, the concept of justice cannot be understood apart from the concept of human wisdom, and that to understand human wisdom we have to have extensive experience (hence a long life) and some idea of human happiness. Before we know the nature of justice, we must first know the nature of human wisdom. And before we know what is human wisdom, we must first know what is human happiness. Hence, in a vague and general way, at the start of the *Republic*, Plato introduces his readers to the concepts of justice, wisdom, and human happiness through the behavior and setting of the characters and their questions.

Failure to recognize these things about Plato's method makes it impossible for anyone fully to abstract, hear, and appreciate what Plato says in the *Republic*. And failure to hear what he says is often due to weak and un-philosophical reading skills, not to our inability to comprehend the concepts involved.

When we start a book's specific reading, we have to survey the book a second time, in relationship to our already-existing outline. This time we look for significant names and words, and their order of appearance in each sub-topic area. We look for such names and words insofar as they introduce problems, questions, definitions, and arguments. This is crucial to do when reading a difficult book for enlightenment because we read such books as students listening to teachers, as intellectual inferiors listening to people who know something difficult that we do not. In this kind of reading, we need to acquire information that is, as Adler is fond of saying, *over our heads*. Such information appears within the text as a problem in need of solution. The problem is always introduced directly, by simply stating it as a problem, or indirectly, through a question (a *request* for information) or a character who asks a question or states a problem.

Teachers and students solve difficult problems through reading by answering questions, discovering information, through explanations. Definitions and examples compose explanations. When we combine definitions and a complex of examples, we construct an argument. Definitions, in short, are psychological tools of identification, mental tools by which we cluster things together and identify them as members of a group. Hence, definitions derive their identifying elements from the things to which apply them. For example, we derive the definition of a philosopher from an observation and knowledge of the behavior of human beings such as Socrates, Plato, and Aristotle. If our definition is any good, it includes something actually in Socrates, Plato, and Aristotle that separates them from other human beings. Therefore, we should be able to use this common element to identify them all together and, simultaneously, to separate them from other people who do not possess this element. We should be able to apply it as a tool for precise identification to the individuals from which we supposedly abstracted it.

After we abstract a definition from a number of individuals, we commonly call these individuals "examples." And using a definition in this way generally constitutes testing the definition by examples. Generally, we call this act of abstracting a definition from individuals and testing it through examples a rational argument, or an explanation. And, we commonly call a "criticism" or "criticizing an argument" the act of testing the definition by examples and concluding whether the definition, or the example, is any good.

We become philosophical readers by practicing this act of criticism. Hence, philosophical reading always involves reading through use of definitions that we abstract from and apply to examples in relationship, or not, to individuals and characters. For this reason, if we want to become powerful and critical readers, once we decide that we are reading difficult material for understanding, we must find the names of significant characters, main questions, crucial words and phrases that introduce major definitions, the examples to which we apply these definitions, main problems, major arguments, and central criticisms.

An easy way to do all this in a specific reading of the text is to consider this type of reading to be mainly a hunt for definitions and their order of appearance. Once we find the main definitions of a work and their order of appearance, in general, we have located a book's main topics of conversation and the way the author connects them.

Again, we can find a simple example of this in Plato's *Apology*. Without reading this dialogue, many people know something about the topic Socrates' formal trial in Athens. Socrates is the first character to speak in this work. He tells his audience that he is reacting to the very persuasive depiction of him made by his accusers in their formal indictment against him. He adds that the content of this depiction consisted of many lies of different degrees of magnitude, which, he says, almost caused him to forget who he was. He maintains that his accusers told one greatest lie about him, that he was an eloquent speaker. He states he will immediately refute this claim as soon as he opens his mouth. Just after Socrates says this, he focuses his listeners' attention on the word "eloquent" as it applies to him and to others, especially his accusers. He says that the word "eloquent" can mean one of two things: (1) to use fancy, ornamented words and phrases to hide truth, or (2) to use simple and easy words, as he does, in the way someone might speak at a bank or at the marketplace, to reveal the truth. After he distinguishes these two definitions of the word "eloquent," Socrates immediately applies each definition to specific examples: definition one to his accusers and definition two to himself. He points out that he and his accusers are not eloquent in the same sense. He speaks plainly, like a person in the marketplace. So plainly that he is not familiar with the way to speak in a law court, especially since this is the first time he has appeared in one as a defendant. So, he asks the jury to make allowances for his foreign way of speaking and to judge him simply upon the basis of the evidence.

A crucial point to note about Socrates' reaction, which constitutes the first general discussion topic in the *Apology*, is that Socrates' conversation only becomes precisely intelligible to the extent that we read everything that takes place within this conversation in terms of the way Socrates intends his listeners to understand his definitions of "eloquent." Socrates bases his entire argument in this conversation upon his listeners' recognition that he defines "eloquent" in two ways and that he applies these different definitions to two different examples

Once we have identified the crucial elements in a book, we have to mark them off in some way in the text, and record them in their order of appearance under the proper sub-topic section headings in an already-existing outline. For example, specific topics comprise the *Apology*. The main topic is whether Socrates, or his accusers, is a criminal. To answer to this question, Plato engages is seven sub-topics of conversation: A. Socrates' reaction to the formal indictment's depiction of him. B. The Old Set of accusations against Socrates. C. The New Set of accusations against Socrates. D. Further explanation of Socrates' behavior to the jury to help them make an impartial decision. E. The vote and Socrates's offer of a counter-penalty. F. Rejection of the counter-penalty and Socrates' address to those who voted to condemn him (his false judges) and to those who voted to acquit him (his true judges). G. The conclusion. In topic outline, or as part of a table of contents for the *Apology*, we might generally summarize these topics as:

A. Introduction: Socrates reacts to his accusers' depiction of him

B. The Old Set of Accusations

C. The New Set of Accusations

D. Socrates' further explanation of his behavior to the jury

E. The Vote and Socrates' counter-penalty

F. Rejection of the counter-penalty and Socrates' address to:
    (1) those who voted to condemn him
    (2) those who voted to acquit him

G. Conclusion

After we do a specific reading of the Introduction, we do a detailed reading, and make above outline more precise. For example:

A. Introduction: Socrates reacts to his accusers' depiction of him
    (1) Depiction was persuasive
    (2) Filled with many lies of different degrees of magnitude
    (3) Lies so big that he almost forgot who he was
    (4) The worst lie, that he is an *eloquent* speaker, will soon be disproved as soon as he opens his mouth
    (5) An "eloquent" speaker may mean:
        a. someone who uses fine, ornamented words and phrases to hide the truth (his accusers)
        b. someone who uses plain and simple words and phrases to reveal the truth (Socrates)
            1. Socrates will use plain and simple words when speaking to the jury because (a) he only knows how to speak the truth (b) he has never been on trial and is unfamiliar with how to speak in a court of law
            2. He asks the jury to make allowance for his plain way of speaking the way they would for the speech of a foreigner in Athens

As we hunt for definitions to fill in the general outline with specific details, we should recall that sub-topics, conversations, compose, and provide the context for development of, a book. One sub-topic contains the main problem, which makes intelligible the entire work's main topic of conversation. Sometimes, authors state this problem explicitly (for example, in mathematics texts and *how to* books). At other times, we have to hunt for it (for example, very often in philosophical works). In addition, sometimes authors introduce a problem by a question or a character. Sometimes, the character is the problem, as is often the case in dramatic and fictional works. When this is the case, the problem's solution lies in the character's definition. And this definition occurs against the background of development of context, setting, and plot. Moreover, sometimes the problem is a personal experience or emotion (such as, in poetry and plays) that we cannot adequately express verbally but which, much like a painter, sculptor, or musician, an author tries to enable us to share through imaginative and emotional constructions (and other modes of qualifying) through artistic use of words.

E. The Individual, or Most Precise, Reading: Reading by the Numbers

After we have generally and specifically read and outlined a book, we need to read with precision and exactness by filling in all the final details, much in the same fashion that a builder leaves the trim of a house for the final stage in construction. This stage involves as precise and exact understanding of the text as we can achieve. We achieve this by progressively re-reading each sub-topic for a precise awareness of: (1) the questions raised, (2) by whom, (3) in what context, (4) in what order, (5) the problems stated, (6) the crucial words used to unravel the problems, (7) the definitions given to crucial terms in the problems, (8) the examples to which the author applies these definitions, (9) and the criticisms the author gives while applying definitions to examples in light of the immediate problem under consideration and the main problem of the work.

Reading numerically, reading by numbers, is crucial to this stage of philosophical reading. Reading for precision demands that we apprehend as precisely as possible what happens first, second, third, fourth, fifth, and so on, in the text, and to understand how these parts relate to the main problem of the text as a whole. For example, in the *Apology*, after we do a specific outline of each sub-topic of whole text (such as I did above with Plato's introduction), the last thing we must do is use our specific outline as a guide for reading the text with individual detail and precision. We must understand, and, as much as possible, numerically commit to memory, the general outline that we made and use it to understand the organization of the whole work, much like an architect uses a set of blueprints to understand the nature of a house.

Thus, in a final reading of the *Apology*, we will know that Socrates *first* reacts to the presentation of his accusers *before* he talks about the Old Set of accusations. We will know, in turn, that Socrates' examination of the Old set of accusations, *precedes* his treatment of the New Set of accusations, and is *followed* by an address to the jury in which he gives them some additional information about this behavior. Moreover, we will know that, *after* this happens, (1) the jury votes to condemn Socrates to death, (2) he offers a counter-penalty, which the jury rejects, and (3) *then* he addresses those who voted to condemn him and those who voted to acquit him, before *finally* drawing the dialogue to an end.

Knowing all these things in general, in their numerical order of appearance in the text, from" an outline, and using the outline as a blueprint and applying it to the text, we must next make sure we understand *the order of appearance of all the specific parts* of each sub-topic of the outline. For example, in the above treatment of Socrates' reaction to his accusers in the *Apology*, Socrates first says his accusers' depiction of him was persuasive, then that it was filled with many lies of different degrees of magnitude. *Next*, that the lies were so numerous and big that he almost forgot who he was. *Then*, that their worst lie about him was that he is an eloquent speaker, and that he will disprove this as soon as he opens his mouth. *After* doing all these things, *then* he defines the term "eloquent" speaker in two different senses. And he proceeds to apply the definition in one sense to himself and in another sense to his accusers (one as someone who hides the truth behind fancy, ornamented words and phrases, and the other as someone who reveals the truth through plain and simple words and phrases). *After* he does all the preceding things, Socrates *ends* his introduction by explaining how he will speak in simple words that are easy to understand, and he asks the jury to make allowance for his behavior because this is the first time he has been brought to court on criminal charges.

Only after we know all these things in their numerical order of appearance can we make sure that we completely understand what Socrates means, for example, when he uses the word "eloquent" to apply to himself and to his accusers. Or why he asks the jury to make allowances for him. Socrates thinks that the only reason a juror should make allowance for the way he speaks is because a "juror," by definition, is a person with an obligation to be impartial and to judge cases on the basis of the evidence. Hence, if we do not know how Socrates defines a "juror," we cannot appreciate what he says in this part of the text.

We are not able to immerse ourselves in difficult reading and, simultaneously, try to figure out or to look up the meaning of every word in a text. Still, critical reading requires that we read a book according to a precise understanding of the author's definition of technical terms. For this reason, when we do a final and detailed reading of a book, we must pay special attention to apprehending all the general parts of the text according to their order of appearance and the meaning of all the words used in all the definitions. We must make sure that we know the meaning of the definitions used, the specific examples to which they apply, and how all these definitions relate to the main argument of the book.

All this is quite complicated and demands skill. Still, we can simplify the activity. Because every book we read for enlightenment involves use of explanation to solve a main problem, everything else in a difficult book is ordered to solving the book's main problem. For example, in Plato's works, (1) the order of solution of the problem follows the order of appearance of the arguments, (2) the order of appearance of the arguments follows the order of appearance of the application of definitions to examples, (3) the order of application of definitions to examples follows the order of appearance of examples, (4) the order of appearance of examples follows the order of appearance of definitions, and (5) the order of appearance of definitions follows the order of appearance of characters. Or, in Plato's dialogues: first come the *characters* who introduce *definitions*. The definitions generate *examples* to test and explain the definitions. Testing a definition constitutes a rational *argument*. And the ordering of the arguments generates the *solution* of the work's main problem, which we can then evaluate *philosophically* as right or wrong. Hence, to read Plato philosophically we must pay special attention to *the order of appearance of*: (1) characters, (2) the question, problems, and definitions they introduce, (3) the examples to which we apply these definitions, and (4) the way in which we logically order the arguments that result from the application of definitions to examples to solve the book's main problem.

This procedure helps us read any difficult book, not just Plato. If a philosophical work, such as one of Aristotle's, does not introduce problems by characters, then, to read the work philosophically, we have to pay precise attention to the order of appearance of three general elements: (1) the question, problems and definitions the author uses, (2) the examples to which the author applies the definitions, and (3) the way in which the author logically orders the arguments that follow from the application of definitions to examples in relation to the work's main problem.

Making some appropriate changes, we can use a similar method to read other difficult books, such as theoretical works about measurement, works about imaginable experiences and "how to" books.

For example, we can use the same method we used to read Plato to read dramatic work or plays, with one qualification: the main problem in a dramatic work or a play is one or a number of characters in relation to developing events. We have to read such a work against the background of the order of appearance of character development, since this is the way in which dramatic works define characters.

Chapter 6

A BOOK'S GENERAL OUTLINE

A. Why Outline a Book?
Critical Reading as a Dynamic Philosophical Act

In the last chapter, I examined how to read any book. I emphasized that philosophical reading demands that we read by applying an outline to a book. We need to outline a difficult book because, to read it for understanding, we have to comprehend how the precise details and specific parts fit together to make a whole. We do at least two things when we outline a book: (1) narrow down our general understanding of the text through use of an imaginary guideline, and (2) abstractly apprehend the parts of a text as ordered to the whole.

When we read in this way, we follow our natural order of learning. When we learn we always add to knowledge through vague contact with an initially sensible thing. Without miraculous intervention, not even the greatest genius ever learns anything, in its most minute details, all at once, upon initial contact. Learning develops progressively. We first become familiar with something in general. Then, specifically. Finally, precisely, in individual detail.

To know something, we apprehend many acts of a whole as multiple parts. First generally. Next specifically. Lastly, in detail.

By practice, we can habituate this natural method of human learning, and, eventually, develop an art of learning. In doing so, we take the many acts of one whole thing and apprehend them as *many unit parts*. We start to understand the precise behavior of individual things by identifying this behavior generally and specifically. We learn habitually in terms of a one and a many. As we become habitually enlightened about things that, at first, we found difficult and only apprehended vaguely, we start to acquire skill. We begin to learn as liberal artists. When we start to wonder about these difficult things through explicit, habitual, and logically consistent application of defined principles, we begin to learn according to abstract philosophical reasoning.

Hence, as the ancient Greeks rightly understood, all philosophical learning involves the problem of *the one and the many*. Not all reasoning is philosophical. Philosophy developed among the ancient Greeks only after they started to view sensible objects abstractly, in a logical fashion, as so many instances of solving problems through logically reasoned explanations of the complex behavior of a one whole thing by the many part ones, or principles, that composed it.

Ancient philosophy attempted abstractly to understand the source, or principle, of the complicated behavior of something in terms of a general and specific understanding of the thing's contents. This made ancient philosophy critical reasoning. It involved becoming enlightened about why and how apparently inscrutable things did what they did. It used abstract explanations of the sources of such acts in terms of a one related to a many, and a part related to a whole.

In critically reading a book, this procedure involves understanding a sensible thing in terms of its contents. These contents relate to the book as many part ones to a whole one, or as parts to a whole. This method also involves habitually engaging in a difficult reasoning process, that enables us to explain precisely what an author intends to say, and why and how it is said. This is difficult, abstract, and logically ordered reasoning, in which we unify a book's contents as parts to a whole and many part ones to a whole one.

Only philosophy employs all these different and difficult abstract reasoning activities. Critical reading is philosophical mainly because critical reading is abstract intellectual activity that must use general and specific outlines to comprehend how many things are one. Because philosophical reasoning involves understanding a thing's behavior in terms of a thing's general and specific make-up, and because such outlines are imaginative aids to the dynamic and abstract act of thinking about one whole book through its general and specific parts, these outlines are simply part of the abstract and dynamic philosophical act of understanding a whole book (a one) in its most minute details (a many) in terms of its general logical principles (many ones).

Because contemporary schools no longer teach reading in this philosophical fashion, universities are declining and American faculty and students are growing progressively more illiterate. Because we lack the classical philosophical training to read and understand a book in general before attempting to read and to understand it in its most minute and individual details, American students and teachers generally attempt "to put the cart before the horse." They misread difficult books by trying to understand the minute details of what they read before they have a general grasp of their subject. This simple philosophical mistake about reading, not lack of comprehension, open enrollment, curriculum changes, or any other apparently lofty explanation, accounts for the widespread illiteracy in American institutions of higher learning today.

B. What is an Outline?

To understand better why we have to outline a book before we can read philosophically and critically, we need to get a precise understanding of the nature of a book. A book is more than a tool for transporting information: a tool for transporting a writer's memory. Our memories work by ordering or organizing images according to their temporal and spatial position within some imagined, general and specific context and order. Hence, to recall something difficult, we must abstractly imagine what we want to recall within temporal and spatial order and boundaries. In difficult reading, an outline serves as the external physical expression of this abstract and imaginatively-represented order and boundaries

In this sense, then, outlining is a drawing of the contextual order of appearance of things or events. Precisely, outlining is a kind of general, specific, and individual numbering. And reading with an outline is reading to number. We need to outline what we read to identify and number what an author says. Outlining is a kind of linear numbering.

When we outline a book's contents during critical reading, we outline what it talks about, its conversations. Outlining involves numbering a book's conversations.

Books we read for understanding consist of problematic conversations, problems demanding solution. We can only solve these problems to the extent that we answer them or explain them through the application of definitions to examples. Critical reading involves outlining a book's conversations according to the definitions, examples, and arguments that explain its topics: the same method used by ancient philosophers like Plato and Aristotle.

C. The Purpose of General and Specific Outlines

Since outlining involves linear numbering, the main purpose of general and specific outlining is to help us come to know something through the imaginative aid of numbering. We outline to number the general and specific topics of conversation that comprise a book.

We outline books in this way to become progressively more familiar with a book's topics of conversation. To know these precisely, we first have to know them in general. Then, specifically. General and specific outlines give us imaginative aids to familiarize ourselves with conversations generally and specifically before we attempt to grasp their precise details.

This resembles home building. While a buyer might like a builder to start house construction with the trim to finish the job more quickly, no good general contractor proceeds in this way. Once built, we first see a house's trim. Before the trim came to be, the linear foundation, framing, plumbing, heating, and wiring, and the architectural blueprint had to exist. Critical and skillful understanding of a house comprehends the house in terms of the unity of its foundation, framing, plumbing, heating, and wiring, and its architectural blueprints.

Just as the main purpose of a home's "rough" construction is to prepare for application of the trim, so the main purpose of philosophically reading and outlining a book is to prepare for the precise reading. We do general and specific outlines and readings of books because, through them, we can gradually gain precise understanding of a difficult book's fine details. All people with skill have to do their work in some orderly fashion. The orders of time and space in which they work, and the organization of their tools and the materials upon which they work, place this demand upon them. The main purpose of a general reading and outline is twofold: (1) to enable us to identify and understand with precision the most general topics of conversation that comprise a book and (2) to grasp their order of appearance. Similarly, the main purpose of a specific reading and outline of a text is to enable us to identify with precision and understand the parts that constitute each specific topic (the characters, definitions, examples, and arguments) and their order of appearance within their general topics.

D. How to Make a General Outline

In a previous chapter, I explained how to outline a book generally and specifically. Since this is a crucial part of philosophical reading, I will go over it again to tie up any loose ends. Sometimes, outlining a book is difficult. Often, this is because the author has not provided an enlightening title or a table of contents, not because the work is especially difficult. A book's table of contents is a general outline. If we want to acquire skills of outlining books, an easy way to proceed is to look at the table of contents of different books and to start copying these down on a page in a notebook.

A book's table of contents might have no lines or numbers. Still, I say that a table of contents is an outline, and that an outline is a numbered line drawing, because authors usually number tables of contents according to chapter headings. These chapter headings name the most general topics of a book. So, a table of contents is a topic outline. Authors arrange these topics in a spatially ordered table (according to a flat or plane surface, a line, one of the meanings of the word "table"). Hence, even if a table of contents page has no formal lines drawn on it, the contents of the book are arranged one under the other in a linear fashion, since all the words "line up" horizontally across the page and the chapter divisions line up vertically down the page.

After we copy the table of contents in a general, or topic, outline, we need to look up, and turn to, the page numbers to which the various chapter headings refer. In order of appearance, we need to copy the chapter subheadings. For example, the title of this chapter is "A Book's General Outline" The subheadings thus far are: "Why Outline a Book? Critical Reading as a Dynamic Philosophical Act," "What is an Outline?", "The Purpose of General and Specific Outlines," and "How to Make a General Outline." Such being the case, a general outline of this chapter thus far would look like the following:

6. A Book's General Outline
    A. Why Outline a Book? Critical Reading as a Dynamic Philosophical Act
    B. What is an Outline?
    C. The Purpose of Critical Reading and Specific Out lines
    D. How to Make a General Outline

In the above outline, I have ordered the different topics using the numeral "6," and the sub-topics using upper case letters, not numbers. An outline is a "numbered" line drawing. Still, my use of letters to identify sub-topics makes sense because changing from numerals; to letters (upper and lower case) enables me to differentiate between topics and sub-topics while maintaining a consistent numerical progression. When I switch from numbers to letters, I maintain numeral progression because letters of the alphabet are numbered and figured sounds. The letter "A," for example, is the first letter of the English alphabet and the letter "Z" is the twenty-sixth and last. Without the ability to number we would have no alphabet. And, without an alphabet, no English language would exist in which to write and read books. Language formation requires ability to qualify, figure, mathematically number, and imagine sounds as quantified. Hence, application of mathematical measuring skills, habits, arts of the *quadrivium*, enable us to read difficult books with precision by numbering topics within a numbered line drawing that we call an "outline."

When we understand the method and rationale for outlining books, we gain a powerful tool for becoming a philosophical reader. I do not mean that our reading will always be trouble-free. Doing all the things I have indicated in this chapter is time-consuming and difficult, but far less time-consuming and difficult than the illiteracy that attends being an un-philosophical and weak reader.

If a book (such as an ancient philosophical text) lacks a detailed table of contents or a title that precisely reflects its most general topic of discussion, we have to make our own table of contents and title. Doing these things is generally not difficult. First, we have know the kind of book we are reading according to the author's intention, and our motives for reading it. Then we have to look for an order of characters and settings. Next, we have to associate general actions with the characters and the settings (especially, definitions and examples the characters introduce in specific settings). If a book has no characters or settings, then we have to concentrate on locating the definitions and examples the author uses. Authors construct arguments out of definitions and examples. Hence, the argument is the context of definitions and examples.

When we read philosophically for understanding, the words "for example" and "for instance" are crucial terms because they indicate that an author has, in some way, recently given a definition, or presumes that we understand a definition to make an example intelligible. Examples and instances are applications of definitions to real-life or imaginary situations. Hence, they are: (1) a direct reference to a real-life or really existing, actual or potential, specifically corresponding event in the past, present, or future, (2) an analogous reference to a real event, or (3) an imaginary specific or analogous likeness.

To make the above points clearer, once again, let us consider Plato. As a great teacher, Plato constantly used simple examples to clarify his definitions. Plato did this because he understood that we can only form an idea if we can first form an image of what we seek to comprehend.[1] While ideas are born in our intellects, we first conceive them in our imaginations. Strictly speaking, our intellects do not conceive ideas, our imaginations do not imagine, and our senses do not sense. People conceive ideas, imagine, and sense. We first imagine with our external senses and the intellect, and conceive with the imagination and external senses.[2] Hence, we cannot recognize an unfamiliar concept without an extreme example in which we can glaringly recognize its concrete presence. We must first turn to a familiar image to grasp a difficult concept because the image gives birth to the concept. If we cannot see the concept there, we cannot see it anywhere. We know unfamiliar concepts through easily-recalled past or present, real or imaginable, experiences of the same or like kind. Since a definition is an explicit expression of conceptual content, to help us conceptualize and form the definition of a thing, any great teacher refers our attention first to extreme, individual expressions of an unfamiliar concept, contained in familiar real-life experiences of the same kind, compares what we are trying to learn to something *like it*, but of a simpler kind, or calls to our imaginations a fictional likeness in the form of a myth, or analogous likely story.

Given the way we are inclined to acquire knowledge about difficult concepts, if we try to outline a difficult book without the help of an enlightening title and a detailed table of contents, then searching the text for examples in the form of real-life experiences, analogies, fables, and the like, becomes crucial. By studying an author's examples, we can start to get a vague idea of the definitions the author uses, the author's intention, and the arguments under construction. With these in hand, we can start to form a vague idea of the general topics of discussion and their order of appearance in the text. With this material, we can begin to construct a book's general outline.

E. How to Make a Specific Outline

After we read and outline a book in general, philosophical reading involves reading and outlining a work specifically. Specific outlining and reading presuppose that we have identified the book's general topics of conversation. The purpose of specific reading and outlining is to find and number, according to their order of appearance, elements that comprise the contents of a work's topics of conversation: (1) characters and setting (if these are explicitly given), (2) definitions, (3) examples, and (4) arguments or criticisms.

We do not specifically outline and read a book to understand its precise details. We outline and read specifically to gain a still general, but narrower, understanding of work by numbering the contents of the general topics of conversation that comprise the text.

In general and specific outlining, we primarily attempt to understand the general details of the work by numbering them according to their order of appearance. For example, in the current chapter of this book, a general and specific outline of the first two sections above looks like this:

6. A Book's General Outline
    A. Why Outline a Book? Critical Reading as a Dynamic Philosophical Act
        (1) Previous chapter emphasized
            a. how to read any book
            b. that philosophical reading demands reading by applying an outline

        (2) We need an outline to understand books that
            a. are difficult to read
            b. we want to understand in precise detail

        (3) An outline helps us do at least two things:
            a. narrow down our understanding of a text
            b. abstractly to apprehend textual parts as ordered in relation to a whole

        (4) When reading with help of an outline, we learn naturally by
            a. adding to our knowledge through contact with sensible things
            b. progressively specifying what we know, starting with the most general and

going to the most detailed

c. apprehending many acts of a single whole in terms of its multiple unit parts

d. becoming habituated in something after gaining experience of it

e. habitually trying to solve problems through explicit, abstract, and logically consistent application of defined principles (by beginning to l earn philosophically)

(5) Habitual reading in this way is philosophical because:

a. philosophy is a form of reasoning that involves wondering how to solve a problem in terms of the one and the many

b. philosophical reasoning initially begins with sense apprehension of some sort of behavior of some one thing that is difficult to understand and that we try to comprehend by explanation application of abstract and logical reasoning to consider part ones, principles, as making up a whole

c. such reading tries to understand a sensible thing in terms of its contents, that relate to the book as many part ones to a whole one, or as parts to a whole, and according to a reasoning process that:

1. is habitual
2. involves difficulty
3. enables us to explain what and how an author intends to state
4. involves abstract and logically-ordered reasoning in terms of the problem of the one and the many

d. only philosophy requires use of all

these different and difficult reasoning activities

(6) Critical reading must employ outlines because
    a. philosophical reasoning involves understanding the behavior of something in terms of that thing's general and specific makeup
    b. such outlines are imaginative aids to the dynamic and abstract philosophical act of thinking about a whole book in terms of its general and specific parts

(7) In the author's opinion, contemporary American universities are declining, and American faculty and students are becoming progressively more illiterate because:
    a. contemporary schools no longer teach reading in this philosophical fashion
    b. teachers and students lack the philosophical training
        1. to read and understand a book in general before
        2. attempting to understand it in its most minute and individual details
    c. we attempt "to put the cart before the horse" by trying to understand the precise details of what we read before we have a general and specific understanding of a text

(8) Consequently, the main cause of widespread illiteracy today in American colleges and universities is a philosophical mistake about learning, not
    a. open enrollment
    b. curriculum changes
    c. any other seemingly lofty explanation

B. What is an Outline?
- (1) An external physical expression of imaginatively-represented, abstract, general and specific context for contents of a book
  - a. a book is a tool for transporting
    1. information
    2. memory of a writer
  - b. the human memory works by ordering and organizing images according to their spatial and temporal position within an imagined general and specific context
    1. to remember something, we have to put it into an imaginative, general and specific, temporal and spatial context
    2. in reading, an outline serves as the external physical expression of this imaginative context

- (2) An outline is
  - a. a line drawing of the contextual order of appearance of things or events
  - b. precisely speaking, an outline is a way of general, specific, and individual numbering of topics

- (3) Reading through use of an outline is reading
  - a. by the numbers
  - b. to identify what an author says and number it
  - c. is linear numbering

- (4) In critical reading, we outline the contents of a book
  - a. a book's contents consist of conversations
  - b. we outline conversations
    1. a book's conversations consist of

(a) problems in demand of a solution because
(b) we can only understand problems to the extent that we answer them through explanation (the application of definitions to examples)

(5) Hence, philosophical reading involves outlining a book's conversations according to the definitions, examples, and arguments that explain its topics

F. Reading a Book to Understand its Precise Details

In critical reading, after we specifically outline a book, we need to make sure that we understand the words that make up the definitions contained in the work's main topics of conversation. To do this we have to consider, precisely, whether the definitions that the author gives in the different topics of conversation are any good. We do this by considering how the author applies a definition to individual examples and also by critically evaluating the author's success. If an author's argument is any good, the given definitions should help us precisely identify the things to which the definitions apply. if this does not happen, then something is wrong with the author's argument. Either the definitions are good and the examples are bad, the examples are good but the definitions are bad, or the definitions and the examples are bad.

Since this is the last stage of a philosophical reading, this involves critically reading all parts of a book in relation to the whole. When we assemble things we have just purchased, we first unpack all the merchandise, lay it out in front of us, separate the different pieces, join them together with the screws provided, and wait to the very end of the job to make sure that every part is in its right place before we tighten the screws. So, when we read philosophically, before we test all the arguments of a book to determine how well they fit together, and how well they unify the author's main argument, we first separate all the pieces of each of the arguments (the words, definitions, and examples), and tie them together loosely, before we finally test how tightly they fit.

The final test is the most necessary. Here we determine whether the author has solved the problem, in the same way that a mechanic determines whether a car will run by trying to start it. Hence, once we are sure that we precisely understand how an author uses the words that make up the definitions of the authors' arguments, then we must consider whether we understand all the definitions in their entirety. To determine this, we have to look at each definition against the background of the examples to which the author applies it. This enables us to see whether we can identify the examples with precision through use of the author's definition. If so, then the author has one good argument. Whether the author's book is good. however, requires that the main argument be good. A book read for enlightenment is good for us if it increases our knowledge by answering a main problem an author proposes to solve. Hence, a good argument contributes to making a good book when it fits together with the other arguments of the book to construct an integrated and logical whole.

For example, consider, again, Plato's *Apology*. In that work, the main problem under consideration is the complicated issue of who is the real criminal: Socrates, or Socrates' accusers and his judges? The whole force of the argument that Socrates is not the criminal depends upon the definitions of a "criminal," "corruption of youth," "impiety," complete and partial "atheism," a "lawful accuser," a "concerned citizen," a "judge," an "innocent citizen," and whether we can most precisely and exactly identify Socrates or his accusers as a criminal through the application of these definitions to the respective ways the characters conduct themselves. In this work, Socrates, his accusers, and judges agree that a criminal is an intentional wrongdoer of an injustice damaging to the good of the city. Initially, Socrates' accusers attempt to define him as criminal because, in a way, they contend that his behavior has defined him as impious (or irreligious) and a corruptor of youth. Socrates' main accuser contends that he brought Socrates to court because he, Meletos, is a "concerned citizen." Meletos and his allies contend that Socrates corrupts the youth of Athens because Socrates is an atheist. Purportedly, Socrates corrupts the youth through his atheism. The given definitions supposedly link Socrates to the definition of being a criminal because criminals are intentional wrongdoers of injustices that damage a city's good. If Socrates' accusers cannot identify Socrates' behavior in terms of these definitions, upon the basis of their argument, they cannot logically establish that he is a criminal.

In the dialogue, Meletos claims that he has brought the suit against Socrates because he, Meletos, is a concerned citizen, the opposite of a criminal. Socrates thinks that the term "concerned citizen" does not accurately define Meletos' behavior. Socrates maintains that "criminal" more accurately identifies Meletos' activities. Socrates contends that he is not an atheist or a corruptor of the youth, and that Meletos, far from being a concerned citizen, is a criminal because Meletos has intentionally brought a frivolous prosecution against Socrates in an intentional misuse of the court. Based upon the evidence, Socrates thinks that his judges, if they fulfill the definition of judges, should find him innocent.

In the *Apology*, the main argument and definition virtually contain all the secondary arguments and definitions. We can only identify Socrates or his accusers as criminals if they did the things that define them to be a criminal. The crucial point is that every difficult book is one large argument made up of one large definition from which we draw one large conclusion. Hence, to understand and read a difficult book as intended by the author we must find the author's main argument and state it in a definition in terms of its sub-arguments. When we have finished reading a difficult book philosophically, we should be able to define it in one or a few sentences in terms of its main topic of discussion in light of the arguments that support it, much as I did above when I defined the topic of the *Apology* in terms of the question "who is the real criminal?" and then proceeded to give the alternatives in light of the way Plato defined and argued about these individuals within the dialogue.

A book's main argument answers the book's main question. To find the main argument, we must find the main question or problem of the book. We find the main problem by discovering what one problem or question the author most wants to answer. The main question is that one question or problem to which all the other questions and problems of the book relate, that unifies all the other arguments, examples, definitions in the work. Another way to find the main question or problem is to find the conclusion of the book. A book's conclusion completes its main argument by answering its main question. Just as a book's main argument and definition virtually contain all the secondary arguments and definitions, so, a conclusion virtually contains the whole book. From the conclusion, we can find the trail of all the secondary arguments, definitions, and examples that constitute the parts that lead up to and establish the main argument.

After we do a final, detailed reading of a book, critically evaluate it in terms of its definitions, examples, and arguments, and define the main topic in one or a few sentences in light of its main arguments, we have, largely, finished our philosophical reading. Only one thing remains, one final change in our outline: constructing general and specific outlines as a combination of topic and sentence outlines. To facilitate our ability to recall the material from our outlines, the last thing we need to do is to reduce our sentence and topic outlines to a few sentence summary of the book. Once we do this, we have a powerful philosophical tool for present learning and future recollection and application.

Chapter 7

PHILOSOPHICALLY READING THEORETICAL MATTERS

A. Different Definitions Make for Different Reading

In the preceding chapters, I spoke of three general rules for philosophically reading any difficult book. Since these rules apply to difficult books, they also work with easy readings. If we can read something more difficult, we can read something less difficult. In easy reading, we do not have to apply these rules as rigorously.

While three rules of philosophical reading apply to reading all difficult works, they do not apply in the same way. All difficult works written for enlightenment are made up of definitions and arguments. All of them set out to solve a difficult problem by means of proof. All proof involves using arguments. And definitions make up all arguments. We cannot compose a difficult, enlightening book without using definitions as their building blocks. When we read difficult, enlightening works, we must know the nature of the work, which the definitions reveal to us, and our main motive for reading it.

Theoretical, practical, mathematical, and imaginable definitions are not identical. To determine how to read a book philosophically we need to pay special attention to the type of definitions that the author uses. We do this by recognizing what and how the author defines.

B. How We Define Theoretical Works

In theoretical works, we consider something that, in some way, really or imaginatively, already exists. A theoretical reader reads mainly for enjoyment or enlightenment, not to put the knowledge gained to immediate practical use. Really or imaginatively, theoretical definitions consider their subjects as finished wholes. We primarily achieve theoretical definition through an act of observation, not of construction or reconstruction, although we might have to perform such practical acts in theoretical knowing in much the same way as we have to make observations in primarily practical ways of knowing. We define a book as theoretical, practical, or whatever, by what, how, and why we primarily read, not by secondary goals and methods that we employ.

C. How to Read Historical Work

Consider a subject like history. Today, many people would consider history to be primarily theoretical, not practical. Yet modern history developed during the Renaissance, as part of the practical activity of political debaters, or orators. Hence, we can study history theoretically and practically.

Whether history be a theoretical or a practical discipline, it always involves reconstruction of the past through use of imaginative weaving of past records. Consequently, historical study considers imaginable and practical experiences.

When we philosophically read history theoretically for enlightenment, our main motive is to consider the way a historian has reconstructed the past so we can understand and evaluate the way the historian achieved this reconstruction. History's subject is the imaginatively reconstructed past, based upon existing records from which to imagine and reason about the past.

This means that, precisely speaking, historical definitions are imaginative and artificial reconstructions about the past as past, not theoretical observations of the past as present. Historical definitions resemble imaginative dramatic reconstructions of events that might be, could be, and so on. A theoretical historian forms these practical and imaginative reconstructions to explain the past as past, not to reconstruct it in the present. A practical historian might use historical definitions to persuade those in the present to learn a practical lesson from history. In this sense, the practical historian is a rhetorician, orator, moralist, or political writer.

The main question of a historical work concerns a past event that is difficult to understand and reconstruct. Hence, the historian considers the past as past and problematic. The historian's art recreates and reconstructs the past to explain something problematic about it. History, therefore, like philosophy, begins in wonder about difficult things to understand.

To solve a historical problem or question, the historian must view the past from the standpoint of the possible future. The historian must consider something that did, but did not have to, happen, and identify the causes that made it come to be.

A good example of this approach is the classical, historical work by Luigi Guicciardini about the sack of Rome in 1527.[1] Rome was sacked in 1527, one of the many times it was pillaged over the centuries. Historians often refer to this attack as a watershed, marking the end of the Renaissance. Guicciardini, the historian, recognized that Rome's fall in 1527 was a unnecessary. As unnecessary, Guicciardini wanted a main explanation to understand this main question or main problem. To achieve this, he had to define Rome's fall as the conclusion of an ordered series of events, each of which, he argued, largely resulted from the cowardice, greed, and foolishness of the Roman people.

Guicciardini's approach presumes that the main event he wishes to explain requires practical, not theoretical, definition. When we consider this event from the perspective of the past, Rome's fall could have been, but was not, averted. If it was preventable, Guicciardini wishes to know why it was not prevented. Guicciardini works with the records at hand like a Renaissance artist, rhetorician, and humanist. And he concludes that the foolish and corrupt behavior of the Roman people was the main reason Rome's fall occurred.

Guicciardini thinks that what defines the Roman people (the principles of foolishness, greed, and cowardice) ultimately defines the conclusion (the fall of Rome). He thinks his definitions and arguments relate as means to an end. He views them, largely, as a recipe, or sequentially-ordered steps, or parts, by which we come increasingly closer to producing an end, or whole, in the same way that by joining parts together in a certain order we come increasing closer to completing a whole.

To understand this work, therefore, we must find the book's main problem (why Rome fell when it did not have to) and the main definition of the Roman people as greedy and corrupt fools. Then, we have to follow the author's detailed application of his definition of the Roman people, in example after example (and, therefore, argument after argument) until we arrive at the Rome's fall. Before the fall, we find a progressive leaning in the direction of toppling. For, before a fall occurs, something moves in the direction of falling. Hence, the series of events fit together like parts of a whole painting. And, once we have produced the whole, we can read it, and critically evaluate it, as hanging, or not hanging, together on the basis of the way the author assembled the parts.

Some readers might object that I misunderstand history and the way to read it when I use a Renaissance scholar like Guicciardini as an example of a historian. This author wrote in the Renaissance tradition of a rhetorician. I answer that Guicciardini's rhetorical writing style does not alter the proper way to read history. While, like many, and perhaps most, historians, he reconstructs the past for purposes of political commentary and persuasion, in so doing, he does not entirely abandon historical method. He subordinates it to rhetorical and political concerns. Still, his work's historical method remains unchanged: imaginatively to reconstruct the past out of existing records at hand to explain a main, but contingent, social, cultural, political, or earthly-related problem, in terms of the past events that caused it. Knowing whether the historian we are reading wishes principally to reconstruct past events to understand them or for some further practical purpose helps us make a final, critical evaluation of the work. These goals might enhance, detract from, or not significantly alter a historian's objectivity. And we should be aware of such influence when we criticize the work as a whole.

From the more specific and practical point of how to read a historical work for enlightenment, we read it the same general way we do any other difficult work. We must first identify and outline the most general and specific topics of discussion, and pay specific attention to author's order of definitions and the examples to which these definitions apply. Furthermore, knowing that we are reading a historical work means that we should look for historical definitions. Since definitions are simply tools for the general identification of something, historical definitions aim at identifying some important occurrence in the past to recreate how it took place simply to understand it or learn a practical lesson.

With respect to reading contemporary historical texts, contemporary historians usually give us a lot of help. Generally, today, history books come with very detailed tables of contents and bold-faced sub-topic divisions on many pages in each chapter. Usually, authors precisely state the main topic at the start of the book and clearly relate it to the book's conclusion. Contemporary historians usually pay close attention to chronology, and often associate this with something else, such as, some president's administration, a king or queen's rule, or a leader or exceptional individual (an educator, inventor, or artist; or a war and heroes and villains). Hence, when we read historical works, we have to put historical events, historical definitions, and examples, within a wider setting of time, place, and character development, just as we do when we read a play.[2]

D. How to Read Other Theoretical Works

Thus far, I have examined, in some detail, how to read two types of theoretical books, historical and philosophical. I have stressed that, when we read any difficult work, we need to understand our subject, method, and the author's order of definitions, examples, and arguments. I have done these things because we often find it difficult to read theoretical works with skill.

In the West, this difficulty partly results from a long, complicated, and confused history related to the growth and development of arts and sciences. For example, among the ancient Greeks, disagreements arose about the nature of philosophy. During the early

Middle Ages, many Greek philosophical works were not available to Western scholars. As a result, Medieval thinkers generally confounded philosophy, wholly or partly, with the trivium of the liberal arts (grammar, rhetoric, or logic). To complicate matters, Medieval thinkers generally studied philosophy within the context of theology. Hence, they often conflated philosophy with the liberal arts and confounded all this with theology. In the thirteenth century, thinkers started to get a better grasp of classical. philosophy. But, shortly after this happened, different events issued in the Renaissance. Renaissance thinkers continued the medieval conflation of philosophy with grammar, rhetoric, or logic, especially with rhetoric and poetry. Ancient Greek philosophers generally considered philosophy to be a study of the causes of the behavior of things through knowledge first derived from the senses. Modern philosophers generally view philosophy as a logical, grammatical, rhetorical, or mathematical system of ideas or feelings. And they view people and events as trains of thoughts or feelings.

This confusion about the nature of philosophy has had dramatic effects upon a number of other disciplines, including theology, sociology, psychology, and anthropology. For this reason, today, thinkers in these disciplines often cannot identify precisely what is their subject matter of study and tell us how they study it. Theologians, philosophers, sociologists, psychologists. and anthropologists today have trouble determining whether they practice an art, science, or something, perhaps, in between. Still, they apparently think they are involved in higher education because they deal with systems of ideas about which they reason logically, persuasively, and, at times, mathematically.

I mention these points to forewarn readers about the way these disciplines tend to work today. A crucial point for a critical reader to understand because, at times, when we attempt to read something difficult we will mistakenly blame ourselves for an inability to comprehend an author's meaning.

Since most contemporary philosophers, theologians, and social scientists think that their work involves constructing ideal logical systems, we should read them as ideal system builders, not as expositors of causes at work in the real world (like Plato and Aristotle). Most contemporary philosophical works are imaginative reconstructions written to unify ideas into a logically consistent belief system. Hence, they resemble paintings or symphonies composed of ideas, dramas made up of character development, or historical or rhetorical works designed to persuade through their impressive organization. They are not primarily designed to convey information about the real workings of the world in which we live.

When we read most contemporary philosophical or social scientific works, we should avoid looking for some real subject being defined as the primary topic of discussion. Often, what an author defines is imaginary. David Hume gives us a good example of this in his *An Inquiry Concerning Human Understanding* when he makes the following comment about "the truths demonstrated by Euclid." He says: "Though there never were a circle or a triangle in nature, the truths demonstrated by Euclid would forever retain their certainty and evidence."[3] Obviously, when Hume says this, he must be thinking of an imaginary Euclid, not the living, breathing, organic being who once lived on the earth. If Euclid, the organic being, had never thought of circles or triangles in nature, no Euclidean idea of such beings would ever have existed. Without really existing circular and triangular things Euclidean truths would not last for an instant, much less than forever. For they never would have come into being in Euclid's mind.

Obviously, in the above instance, Hume projects imaginary constructs onto the physical world in which he actually lives and knows as an organic being. Most modern and contemporary philosophers work similarly. For example, the Father of Modern Philosophy, Renè Descartes thought he proved himself to be a pure spirit closely connected to an extended being that he called his body. After doing this, he imagined the sort of world which he inhabited.

Descartes's motives for his method are historically and philosophically important. I need not go into detail to make the point that, when we read most modern and contemporary philosophical, theological, and social scientific works in the West, we will understand them better and get less confused by them if we approach them as complicated and logically organized works of fiction or rhetoric that tell an imaginary story through use of technical definitions. Hence, when we read a modern or contemporary sociological, anthropological, or philosophical work, we should not presume that the author has scientifically established the existence of a certain form of human association. We should be more concerned about how the author technically defines this form of association and how, in light of this definition, it is logically consistent to conclude that other types of associations arise. Hegel does not establish the existence of an absolute Spirit, the evolution of which constitutes history, and Marx never abstracted his dialectic of history from a thorough and detailed examination of the way societies developed in the past, any more than anthropologists who contend that cave men beat their wives have established this from a detailed observation of primitive cave psychology. Instead, they all project a fiction onto reality and attempt to make the reality fit the fiction.

Whether this approach has any intellectual merit is not my concern in this work. My concern is that we avoid confusion when we try to unravel the parts that constitute the makeup of modern and contemporary theoretical works. The best advice I can give readers is, first, to read these works as if they were reading fiction. Then to look for the author's definitions as building blocks of logically consistent systems of ideas. Again, when we read any difficult work, we have to focus attention on definitions and examples. We need not worry about whether the societies that contemporary anthropologists study ever really existed, or whether a psychological element like the *Id* is a true analysis of the human psyche. Whether an *Id* exists is no more important for understanding Freud than whether Zeus really existed is important for understanding Homer.

When we read contemporary theology, philosophy, sociology, psychology, and sociology texts, just as when we read history texts, we should look at the title and the conclusion, the table of contents, and the boldfaced sub-topics that appear in the different chapters. On the basis of these, we need to find the main topic of discussion, construct general and specific outlines. Then, in light of. these outlines and using them as guidelines, we have to read the book for a precise understanding of its most minute details.

When we read modern and contemporary philosophical texts, we should not expect to increase our understanding of the causes at work in the world in which we live. Also, at times, these books have no detailed tables of contents to make them more easily comprehensible. When they do, we should use them to find the main topic of discussion and do all the other things that we normally do when critically reading of a book. Remember that these works resemble fictional epics that construct worlds of ideas, or logical systems. To understand them, we must find the author's main definitions or ideas from which other ideas and definitions flow like Athena from the head of Zeus.

Recall that words, images, and ideas are technical tools of any liberal artist. As a result, all professional intellectuals often employ words in technical ways, altering the commonly used definitions we employ in everyday forms of speech. When an ancient pagan Greek philosopher like Plato and a Medieval Christian theologian like St. Thomas Aquinas use terms like "good" or "bad," "true" or "false," "being" or "non-being," "same" and "different," "real" or "unreal and so on, we should not automatically presume that they do so in the same way we do in ordinary conversation. Plato thinks that the word "good" principally means being one, complete, and unchanging. Hence, to the extent that anything is not complete, one, and unchanging, Plato thinks it is not good. Moreover he maintains that the true is the precise. If something is not precise, in a way, for Plato it is false. For this reason, at times, Plato will say that our senses are not true (meaning that they are not precise), but what they report is, nevertheless, real.

To someone coming from a Jewish, Christian, or Muslim tradition, to say that something can be false but real sounds absurd. The God of Jewish Scriptures looks upon the world of change and says that it is good. And for Jews, Christians, and Muslims when something goes out of existence it does not simply become different. It is completely annihilated. The idea of total and complete annihilation is as incomprehensible to an ancient Greek like Plato as is the notion of creation out of nothing. If we were to ask an ancient Greek where everything that now exists ultimately came from, the normal response would be something like, "From what was here before"—not "God created it out of nothing."

This definitional difference is crucial to understand when we try to read a work for enlightenment, especially works written in alien times and places. We have to take special care to understand how an author defined terms and how an audience tended to understand them. For this reason, when we read a difficult work for precise understanding we must try to grasp an author's definitions against the background of the given examples, and translate into our own words definitions that we think we might currently use in ordinary conversation to identify an author's example. When we put the author's examples into our definitions, we start to translate the author's ideas into contemporary and more familiar terms. In this way, we make difficult work easier to understand.

Chapter 8

PHILOSOPHICALLY READING MATTERS OF MEASUREMENT

A. A Short History of Measurement

Mathematics and experimental science are two of the most problematic areas of contemporary reading. A main reason that many people today are "math-o-phobes" has little to do with their mathematical ability and a great deal to do both with the generally poor way in which we teach these subjects and our general inability to read philosophically. In this chapter, I do not intend to eliminate this phobia overnight. I intend to give a reader some essential tools for philosophically reading such works by gradually increasing understanding and confidence.

To eliminate this unnecessary fear and establish some philosophical reading habits regarding such works, let us consider the general nature and historical development of the mathematical and experimental sciences in the West. For human beings to be curious about their surroundings, to engage in exchanges with one another, and to measure things for different reasons are common and normal. For example, we like to measure things so we can exercise choice. But, often, we confront obstacles, of different magnitudes, to exercising choice. For this reason, we generally consider ability to remove obstacles as good. At times, we use tools to remove these obstacles. Hence, we often consider the ability to know how to acquire, fashion, and use tools to be a human good. Obtaining, fashioning, and using tools often demands use of mathematics. We need mathematical know-how to acquire, fashion, and use sophisticated technologies. We need to measure things, therefore, to obtain and fashion tools, to make clothes and shoes, to build homes, to make automobiles and monetary exchanges with one another, to engage in trade and commerce, to divide land, make war and peace, tax citizens, establish rules of speech, grammar, painting, sculpture, and music, to be able to tell time, learn to speak, read, write, sing and dance, to outline books for critical reading, and to be able to do scientific research.

Since we are living, organic beings, our surroundings, and the materials generally and easily available to us to get and fashion tools, incline us to measure things in a definite order. First, we tend to measure things through our body parts and materials abundantly available, close at hand, and easy to move.

A general history of the origin and development of the measuring art reveals that human beings first started to measure lengths, volumes, time, and weights. We first measured lengths by using body parts, such as a finger, the palm of a hand. and a forearm. Later, we started to use artificial measurements, such as the king's hand size or the size of the king's waist, determined by the length of his belt, to measure a yard length. We first measured time in terms of distance by numbering the cycles of motion of heavenly bodies, such as the sun and moon. We started to measure volumes by using different kinds of plant seeds placed in a container. And we stated measuring weights by a balance scale and objects like seeds and stones.

As Middle Eastern and Western civilizations developed, so, too, did different ways of measuring things in different locations, times, and places. As a result, an increasingly wide lack of uniformity developed in cultural standards of measuring in different times and places. In modern times, as nation-states started to develop and as international communication, exchange and trade grew, so, too, did a need for uniformity and precision in use of weights and measures. Consequently, nations held international conventions at which they made agreements to encourage mathematical and physical scientists to raise the activity of measuring to that of an art and science.

As a result of a request made by the French National Assembly to have the French Academy of Sciences "deduce an invariable standard for all the measures and all the weights," near the end of the eighteenth century a crucial international convention convened to discuss developing uniform international standards of weights and measures. The efforts of this meeting produced a uniform, international, minimum standard for all mathematical measures, the metre (meter).[1]

We arrived at this standard by convention, not nature. Somewhat arbitrarily, we agreed upon, and, eventually, through international agreements, internationally accepted the meter as an international base unit measure. Choice of the meter as a measure related to an approximation of part of the earth's circumference, was somewhat, but not entirely, arbitrary. We could have chosen a part of the circumference of a king or queen's waist. But this might have proved politically embarrassing and diplomatically complicated. International politicians would have had to agree upon which king's or queen's waist to use. And some rulers might not have wanted their waist to be used at all.

Another point to note about developing an international standard of measuring is that the uniform, international, mathematical standard of measure is a small length of a natural body, a minimum physical length. We first derive all other mathematical ideas from the idea of bodily length just as we first derive all letters and words from the making of small, figured sounds. Just as we can imagine spoken letters and words through figured lines that we can use as additional means of communication, so we can imagine minimal physical lengths in different ways to measure things, such as pluralities, volume, weight, density, light, speed. time, force, and velocity.

In devising conventional, international measuring standards our first unit measures must be regular and uniform, and we must consider the way they affect our senses. A main purpose for developing increasingly precise international standards of measuring is to achieve uniformity, especially in trade and commerce, so as to avoid confusion in international exchanges. This means that a main goal of such conventions is to achieve consistently increasing certainty and precision in measuring quantities so as to avoid disputes among people about such things as amounts and weights. The whole purpose for developing an art of measuring at all is so that we can conduct direct acts of knowing quantities in orderly, easy, and error-free ways.[2] Furthermore, to achieve precision of knowing we use natural or conventional measuring tools. Through them we know the quantity of things with precision and certainty. This means that the first, or base, units that we use to measure things have to have a minimum quantity relatively invariable to the senses. By using a small standard, we can measure many things, and more easily. And, by using uniform, regular, and sensibly noticeable standards, our unit measures generate exactness in physical exchanges. Hence, very small changes in uniformity and use of unit measures tend to escape our sensory notice. We do not tend to be troubled by such minor deviations when we seek exactness in measuring things, especially, things that we do not consider of great economic value (like gold and diamonds) or of intense military power (such as explosive chemicals).

B. The Origin and Growth of Mathematical Ideas

The importance of mathematical ideas has increased over the centuries. In the seventeenth century, some discoveries that measuring and mechanical scientists made about the useful role that mathematics can play in developing technologies and helping us precisely understand and control the motion of physical things caused dramatic increase of Western interest in mathematics. Interest in mathematics goes back centuries. It was transmitted to the West primarily through contact with the Middle East, where ancient civilizations became curious about knowing how to measure and number things.

Mathematics started to develop as a liberal art with the ancient Greeks when they noticed that we can know bodily quantity by using divided lines to develop an art of communication and measuring. The Greeks noticed that by cutting, or dividing, a bodily line into parts they were cutting a whole into parts and making a one into many. By dividing a line, we make a plurality of lines. This plurality is of one line separate from another line.

Both these lines have not been further cut. They are undivided. Being undivided, each is one. Put back together, we can imagine these separate ones, considered as equal, to be part of the whole we originally cut. So imagined, the original two-part ones make up the whole. The whole length is thus equal to two equal part ones.

Starting with an extended, one dimensional being (a physical line), we arrive at the notion of a plurality of ones as the starting point from which we start to imagine an activity that, today, we call "counting" or "numbering." By noticing that a cut line produces a plurality of ones, we arrive at the idea of number. A number is, thus, a plurality, or repetition, of ones. Our idea of number does not arise simply from the idea of a plurality alone, however. To arrive at the concept of a number (a unit of measure and knowing), we must recognize that we can cluster pluralities together into an order of equal and repeated unit parts, and can imagine these repeated units (a plurality) as units for knowing other things. For example, just as one inch (an undivided, uniform, equal, regular, and minimum measure of length) is a measure, so are three feet, as one yard (an undivided, uniform, equal, regular, and minimum measure of length). Hence, as numbers, pluralities are ordered, or organized into, imagined, and understood as many equal and repeated ones taken together for the purpose of knowing them together as a whole unit made up of part ones. Hence, one and one *taken together* (as if they were a whole unit made up of equal part ones), not one and one, are two!

Once the ancient Greeks recognized that the idea of number originates when we imaginatively cut an extended, continuous, and dimensional being (a body extended in one direction, a linear body) into parts that we then imagine to be put back together into a whole unit, they had the starting point for developing the art and science of geometry and arithmetic.

This happened as follows. First, they imagined a physical substance as a flexible body stretched in one direction (they imagined a body to be linear). Then they imagined this linear body as if it were made up of part ones (that they called points). Positioned evenly along a line they called these points "straight," unevenly positioned, they called them "angled," or "curved." Imagining a body to be linear in this fashion, they could measure it, and, thereby, know its length with precision by counting the points of its length as parts out of which the whole line was composed. This *measured* length of a body became the mathematical concept of length or mathematical length.

After the ancient Greeks developed the ability to measure a body by means of its extension, or *stretch* in one direction, imagined as if this were an extension of numbered points, they imagined a body to be stretched, or extended, in two directions (between two lines, not two points). And they noticed that they could measure a body stretched in two directions (width) by similarly imagining this length between lines as if it, too, were a numbered whole made up of uniform, regular, straight, equal, and smaller widths. In this way, they came up with the ideas of a surface, square surface, measured width (area), and the unit measure of area, square length (for example, a square inch or a square foot).

After this, the Greeks imagined a body to be stretched in three directions: (1) from one point to another, a linear body; (2) from one line to another, a wide, or surface, body; and (3) from one surface body width to another, a deep body. In this way, they arrived at the ideas of a deep body, measured depth (or volume), and the unit measure of volume, cubic length (for example, a cubic inch or cubic foot).

Once they had finished measuring the extension of bodies through numbered lengths in different directions, the ancient Greeks turned their attention from measuring a body in terms of its internal dimensions to measuring it in relation to its qualities and surroundings. Aside from having extension according to internal dimensions in three directions, all physical bodies have qualities, such as being heavy or light, hard or soft, hot or cold, and of one color or another. In addition, the motions of such bodies have the qualities of being fast or slow. And their actions have the qualities of strong or weak. The ancient Greeks did not develop extensive techniques for measuring the qualities, motion, and action of physical bodies. Archimedes, however, started to develop techniques for measuring weight. Galileo Galilei and Sir Isaac Newton later revived and extended these techniques and extended and developed the modern science of mechanics, that is, more or less, identical with modern physics.

Recall that ancient Roman and Greek cultures depended upon development of machines to conduct and improve building and warfare. They needed engineering skills to build an aqueduct, send a projectile into the air to strike an enemy fortification, or build a city on stilts (such as Venice) and escape the attacks of horsemen, such as invading Huns. These skills involve understanding how to use weights, levers, springs, and other such things, to move difficult materials, such as water and heavy objects. To perform such activities with any precision requires geometrical skill. To move things with physical skill, we have to move things in a specific spatial direction according to specific angles. And we have to be able to imagine a body as extended, heavy (in the sense of gravity), and as having a weighty influence upon its surroundings (a dense body).

The ancient Greeks first arrived at a more mathematically explicit notion that we can imagine weight in terms of a body moving downward, or toward the center of the earth, and in terms of the way it affects its surroundings when Archimedes realized that, when we place a heavy body in water, it displaces a specific quantity of liquid. We can then take this displaced amount of water, place it in a container and, through use of a balance scale, compare its measured weight to the measured weight of the object that displaced it. In this way, mathematicians can arrive at the idea of volume weight, density, a very helpful concept in different forms of building, mechanics, and engineering. This notion begins mechanics as a science.

The idea of density, then, is a mathematical idea that combines the geometrical idea of volume (a cubic container, a measure of length) with that of weight affecting its surroundings by displacing a fixed quantity of something by making it move. Strictly speaking, volume is a geometrical measure employed to number (or know) by containing a body within internal boundaries. Volume as a measure of dense weight, however, is contained weight used to measure displaced volume weight (such as, a heavy person sitting in a bathtub will displace some volume weight of water. When mathematically measured, this amount of water is density).

For the purpose of critical reading, we need to realize that all modern experimental science is a philosophical, mathematical exercise of measuring qualities, activities, and motions. The ancient Greeks primarily developed the arts and sciences of mathematics to measure figured and non-moving quantities, such as triangles, circles, and so on. They did so by noticing that we can measure extended and figured bodies by points, lines, and angles. For example, some ancient geometrician noticed that we can imagine a circle to be cut in half by a straight line of a definite length (a diameter). The circle considered as such is simply a curved line with a definite length (circumference). No matter what is the length of the circular line, if we imagine it to be straightened out and imagine the straight line diameter to be placed next to or on top of the formerly curved line, two I things become noticeable. First, the diameter line is always shorter in length than the circumference line, and the circumference line is always a little more than 'three times the length of the diameter line. Or, mathematically expressed, $C = \pi \cdot D$ or $C = 3.1417 \times D$.[3]

Measuring the circumference of a circle involves nothing especially complicated. It should not cause most of us fear. The formula, however, might intimidate some of us. The formula is shorthand notation, a contraction, of a mathematical definition. And all mathematical definitions concern how to put together smaller quantitative parts to make up bigger quantitative wholes, or how to take apart bigger quantitative wholes and understand them in terms of smaller quantitative parts. Hence, most mathematical concepts are easy to comprehend. For most of us, mathematical reading, not mathematical concepts, is the problem. Understanding how we can read sound with our eyes complicates our difficulty reading books about modern mathematics and experimental science. Before any human being had ever conceived of communicating sound by engraved, or painted, figured lines, most human beings would not have been easily able to conceive how such a thing could be done because they could not imagine how it could be done. Once a person did imagine picturing longer and shorter figured sounds in terms of uniform lines of specific lengths and shapes to which, through training of our memories, we could associate sounds, this complicated transfer could become commonplace, and seem almost innate, not something acquired by long, tedious habit. Similarly, before anyone had ever conceived of applying geometrical principles to measure qualities and activities like heat, light, electricity, and so on, how the whole thing might be done is difficult to imagine.

C. The Major Role Played by Galileo Galilei and Sir Isaac Newton in the Growth of Modern Mathematical Measuring Science

The famous seventeenth-century mathematicians Galileo Galilei and Sir Isaac Newton play a major role within the development of modern measuring science. Galileo and Newton changed the way mathematicians imagined qualities, moving bodies, and activities so that we might measure these realities mathematically, especially through use of geometrical principles. Just as ancient Greek mathematicians developed the art and science of geometry by imagining a body's ability to be stretched in three different directions, that they could measure in terms of the mathematical ideas of length, width, and volume (which measuring they expressed in terms of geometrical rules or formulas), so Galileo and Newton developed modern experimental science, or the science of mechanics, by imagining that moving bodies, qualities, and actions can be stretched in terms of straight lines. Modern physics uses straight lines to measure non-mathematical realities such as motion, speed, velocity, time, distance, volume, weight, mass, force, heat, light, and electricity.

Modern physics textbooks generally identify Galileo as the father of modern science because Galileo first conceived of using straight line motion as the basic means for measuring all motion in the physical universe. For mathematical measuring purposes, Galileo imagined that the natural motion of a body is in a straight line. If it moves in a curved fashion, he thought that some external force (like gravity) must be deflecting it from its straight-line (rectilinear) path. And he imagined that, if friction and gravity have no influence on a body, it will continue to move indefinitely in rectilinear motion. Newton would later use this concept of indefinite rectilinear motion as his first law of motion in his revolutionary *The Mathematical Principles of Natural Philosophy*. Consider, for example, lunar motion, or a spacecraft orbiting the earth. To measure the movement of such bodies, contemporary mathematicians must imagine curved motion as a series of straight lines that approximate a curve. In a way, the whole of modern physics involves developing mathematical formulas that enable us to translate curves, areas, and volumes into straight lines because, strictly speaking, in mathematics, the only way we can measure anything numerically is in terms of straight lines, not curves.[4]

Newton, for example, imagined three dimensions of space and time, as if the space and time were three-dimensional volume containers of a qualified, mobile, acting body. He considered an imaginary three-dimensional body moving in a spatial container in one, uniform, or even, direction from one point of rest to another (that is, imagined to be moving in a straight line) as a body with weight (a heavy body), something we can measure geometrically. Similarly, he imagined a three-dimensional body moving in a spatial container in two, uniform, or even, directions (widthwise), as a dense body. In this way, we can geometrically measure density. Finally, Newton imagined a three-dimensional body moving in a spatial container in three directions (with depth) as a body mass. Like weight and density, we can measure mass geometrically.[5]

To appreciate Newton's accomplishments, we need to realize that he extended the ancient science of geometry to a new area of measuring qualities, motions, and actions. Furthermore, we need grasp that he could do this (1) because the ancient Greeks had been able to imagine physical bodies to be linear and intrinsically stretched in three dimensions, and (2), because of Archimedes' work, that enabled the Greeks to imagine geometrically measured body weight as having a geometrically measurable impact upon spatial surroundings.

D. A Similarity between the Mathematical Measuring Scientist and the Writer

A main point I want to make in this chapter is that we can more easily read works in mathematics and experimental science if we have some familiarity with the general activity that mathematicians and experimental scientists perform and the way they imagine things when they work. Just as we cannot precisely understand what reading and writing require without imagining how we can represent figured sounds to our minds through figured lines, so, unless we start to imagine how it might be done, we cannot understand how we can extend methods of counting lengths in one, two, and three directions by representing bodies through straight lines to counting motions, qualities, and actions. In this respect, the mathematician and writer are quite similar. Like acts of verbal communication, we begin acts of measuring by using sounds (counting) and figured lengths (written numbers). Furthermore, very often counting, especially through use of lines, requires that we first engage in physical activities, such as pointing to individual things, making line drawings, using scales, or rulers, to express the complexity of our activity.

In addition to expressing the complexity of our actions, in activities like writing and measuring, the tools we use act as examples of the definitions of our activities. For example, writing is a form of engraving or drawing for the purpose of lettering. This, however, requires a tool with a specific kind and size of tip and definite qualities. Mathematical measuring, in turn, can involve use of a straight-line ruler, protractors, balance or spring scales, thermometers, barometers, cash registers, calculators, spectrometers, odometers, clocks, and so on. For example, we can define weight in terms of the inclination of one body to exceed another body in the way the body inclines or pushes toward the center of the earth. As such, we can measure body weight through comparison, by means of a balance scale. In another sense, we can define weight as the relative pull or of attraction of the earth upon a body. Then we can measure weight by a coiled spring-hook scale. Hence, when we read mathematical works, or works dealing with experimental science, we must pay attention to what is being measured and the way we measure it, especially to the tools we use to measure.

E. Specific Suggestions About Critically Reading Mathematical Books

Recall that reading is simply a hearing aid for understanding. People understand things by comprehending how, in some way, they are one. This is as true in mathematics as it is in any other kind of human understanding. Mathematicians, however, apprehend unity between things by apprehending everything about which they think through the idea of equality, the one in quantity.

They constantly try to know things by comparing them in terms of their equality. Things, however, can be exactly, or more or less, equal. Compared to another, one thing might exceed it in quantity or be below it. For this reason, as their most basic operations, mathematicians employ the activities of adding, subtracting, multiplying, and dividing. Furthermore, all mathematical rules express some equality. For example, the first rule, or definition, upon which all mathematical reasoning is based is that a whole is equal to the sum of its parts. From this, mathematicians arrive at the ideas that: (1) a part is less than a whole; (2) a whole is more than any one of its parts; (3) when equals are added to equals their results are equal; and (4) if equals are subtracted from equals the remainders are equal. Furthermore, from the meta-physical principle that two things that are the same as a third thing are the same as each other, mathematicians derive the mathematical principle that two things that are equal to a third thing are equal to each other. Using such preliminary truths about quantities and the way they relate, as measuring scientists, mathematicians extend these rules, adapt them to specific kinds of things they measure, and construct different technologies, as extrinsic measuring aids, to speed up, facilitate, and make more precise their measurement of the different things they measure.

In all their efforts, however, mathematicians always aim at one thing: to compare things as parts to wholes in terms of their relative equality or inequality. Hence, the equal sign is the principal tool of understanding that mathematicians use. Parts are on one side of the equal sign. A whole is on the other. The mathematician always seeks to maintain a balance, like a seesaw, between the two through use of practical operations like adding, subtracting, multiplying, and dividing.

For this reason, even though I have said that mathematics is a theoretical science, like all sciences, mathematics involves employing practical operations in a definite order. We do not call sciences "theoretical" because no practical activity takes place in them, any more than we call a science "practical" because no theoretical activity happens in it. Mainly, we call sciences practical or theoretical on the basis of the principal object of desire that we have in view when we engage in one form of knowing in the other. We study theoretically when we study mainly to understand how and why things are and are done, not how and why we do them (the main object of desire for practical study).

If we want to read difficult mathematical works, we must know technical mathematical terms, mathematical jargon, especially those terms that identify basic mathematical operations. Mathematicians have their own conventional shorthand-method of identifying their operations, just as people do in many other activities. To save time and effort, for example, often, waiters in restaurants will call in their orders for specific items on a menu by using their own jargon. It might involve using numbers, or names of celebrities. Hence, they might yell in an order as a "Number 6" or as "Frank Sinatra." This is simply a shorthand for the ordered operation that the waiter is telling the chef to exercise. In the case of a "Number 6," this might mean that the waiter tells the chef to take a hamburger patty out of the refrigerator, put it into a heated broiler, cook it for such and such a period of time, while turning it over every so many minutes, and then to take the cooked material out of the oven, place it on bun, then on a plate, with a pickle and some coleslaw, and ring the waiter after all this is finished. All these activities, in short, are part of the whole operation of ordering a "Number 6."

A crucial point to notice about this activity is that, when we consider every human action with some precision, almost every one is enormously complex and orderly. An action might appear to be simple and un-orderly to people who have not considered the richness of human intelligence, imagination, and habit that produces it. The same is true of mathematical acts.

As a result, for us to expect to become good at doing mathematics when we refuse to become familiar in general with mathematical operations, their order of application, and mathematical jargon, is naive. Like all human activities, all mathematical operations take place in an order of before and after. As simple an operation as adding or subtracting has a condition of numerical equality before and after the operation is applied. To know the action precisely we must have a general familiarity with the order of these before and after operations (such as the rules of commutation, association, and distribution in algebra).

We must also be generally familiar with basic mathematical symbols of equality, inequality, more, less, subtraction, addition, multiplication, and division, and must understand what order of before and after actions these symbols reveal to, or command, us to perform. And we must pay attention to how to perform these specific operations on the specific quantitative material to which we apply measuring science. What are we adding or subtracting, multiplying or dividing? Lines? Angles? Curves? Time or heat considered as linear? Motion as traced on surface squares of graph-paper? Sound imagined as waves? Volume liquids imagined as cubes of weight? Numbers considered as clusters of indivisible cut lines existing in separation one from another? Mathematicians and critical readers of mathematical works must know what are the conventional, minimum, unit measure standards, how mathematicians conventionally define them, and what technologies these measures involve and apply to different measured things. Are we measuring a liquid in liters? A weight in ounces or pounds? A length in meters? inches? feet? yards?

A critical mathematical reader must, also, always be on the lookout for the equality and inequality that any mathematical problem first expresses, and must recognize that, ultimately, we can only get the equality we seek through a simple or complicated mathematical operation involving addition or subtraction, using or not using different technologies for observing and comparing equalities.

General familiarity with what we measure and how we measure it is crucial for doing mathematics and critically reading mathematical works. The major mistake that we make when trying to read mathematical works is bad reading, not bad comprehension or failure to apply some vague act called "critical thinking." We use the poor, uncritical, and un-philosophical reading habit of "putting the cart before the horse," or of attempting to understand in precise detail something with which we have gained no prior general and specific familiarity. Instead of first becoming familiar with mathematical jargon (the words used to symbolize mathematical operations) and mathematical directions, and instead of first looking for crucial words expressing relationships of equality (such as "same" and "equal") and changes from a state of equality (such as "before" and "after") and making sure we understand what mathematical questions ask, we try immediately to answer such questions in fine detail. Not even a genius can learn mathematics in this way. For those of us who happen to be less than geniuses, this approach to learning is naive. The best approach we can take to acquire mathematical skill is to practice critical reading of mathematical problems, including attempting to symbolize what math problems express through their written directions and to express in terms of written directions what mathematical problems state in symbols. When we develop a facility doing such acts, we are well along to becoming critical readers of mathematical works.

F. Specific Suggestions About Critically Reading Books in Experimental Science

Understanding all the points made thus far in this chapter, especially, the points made about the role of Sir Isaac Newton in the development of the modern science of mechanics, helps us to understand how critically to read books dealing with experimental science. In addition, we need to recognize something about the art and science of measuring: strictly speaking, only quantities can be directly measured mathematically, just as, strictly speaking, words are sounds. Nevertheless, nothing prevents us from imagining words as figured lines and communicate more universally and with greater precision through writing and reading. Imagining words in this way does not falsify the message or communication they transmit. What changes is the delivering device, not what is delivered.

These points are crucial for understand what happens in contemporary experimental science and how this study achieves and communicates truth. Experiments and proofs of physical scientists are like proofs and experiments in which we generally engage. Proof in experimental science involves applying mathematical definitions to examples, just as we do in philosophy, history, or any other discipline in which we offer proof for our claims. Proof in contemporary physical science is distinctive in the way it employs imagination and human technology to apply, and test, its mathematical definitions via examples.

This activity is so complicated because the experimental scientist is a mathematical measuring scientist. Mathematicians test the truth of their work by applying their mathematical definitions to imaginary constructs, not by eating what they have baked like a cook, or by playing the stock market like an investment banker. Experimental scientists (chemists, biologists, and physicists) work in an experimental setting because they try abstractly to isolate the material upon which they work from any outside influences that might cause it to deviate from a specific state of rest, motion, or previous qualitative uniformity or equality.

As mathematical measuring scientists, experimental scientists cannot start their work of measuring until they first observe something to be measured. And they have to refer whatever they measure to a state of equality, or evenness—a straight line. From this state of evenness (especially, when they try to measure non-quantitative realities like qualities, motions, and actions), they can start to observe some deviation from being even or equal in terms of increase or decrease. For this reason, all the laws of contemporary physical science express the behavior of their respective subjects in terms of equality, uniformity, and regularity. To make such a law about how to measure a quality, motion, action, and so on, the measuring scientist must observe that the same one kind of thing behaves in an equal way, from which it starts to deviate. *At and from this observed point of deviation, all the laws of contemporary experimental science give definitions, expressed in the form of measuring recipes, for numbering these respective subjects of measurement.* In the physical world in which we live our everyday lives, nothing is perfectly straight, completely at rest, in uniform straight-line motion, or completely uninfluenced by its surroundings so that we can always and with precision determine what causes a thing to deviate from its previous state. Still, without imagining non-quantitative beings in such an equal or even, linear state, we cannot associate mathematical measuring principles with them, just as, with the help of human memory, we associate figured lines with sounds.

Just as the writers write to verify that the procedure of trapping sounds within imaginary lines does not falsify their message, experimental scientists do the same thing, mathematically. Mathematical (measuring) formulas work because they are true. They are true as expressions of correct ways of measuring. Mathematicians verify their truth in the same way they verify measurements about quality, motion. and action: by imaginary tests. Mathematicians do not verify their judgments about measurement by testing them in relation to externally sensible realities, but to imaginary ones. What is true about a mathematically straight line is not necessarily the case about a physical one. No physical line has its points evenly positioned the way the straight line of a geometer does. The geometrician uses the imaginary line, not the physical one, to test geometrical truth. Hence, in modern experimental science, we test physical observations by attempting to replicate in a laboratory imaginary initial conditions of equality and evenness that simply do not exist in our real, physical world.

This experimental method of testing mathematical truth does not falsify the work of experimental scientists any more than the imaginary constructs of the geometer or of the writer falsify their activities. So long as the geometer does not mistake the geometrical line and its mathematical *measuring* principles with the real line with its real principles of extension, the mathematician is not likely to become confused about what is involved in mathematical truth. Just as, so long as the writer does not confuse written with spoken words, the writer will not tend to get confused about what is involved in writing truth. One reason the truths of experimental science are so difficult for many of us to comprehend is that experimental scientists use highly complicated tests to measure generally unmanageable realities. Strictly speaking, mathematical measurement directly applies to bodies extended in space according to three dimensions. Such bodies are things with bulk or magnitude divisible into parts that we can easily stabilize, count, and directly compare to each another. Such is not the case with motion, figure, color, light, heat, and so on. Such realities are not quantities. Not being quantities, they are not normally the things that, historically, mathematicians first started to measure. When a thing's motion increases or decreases we have added and subtracted no parts from its bulk. When we squeeze a rubber ball, its quantity remains un-changed, but its figure alters. When the intensity of a thing's color changes, it does not become bigger or smaller, or altered to another color. And, while heat causes some materials to expand, heat is not what expands. Light alters transparent bodies without increasing or decreasing their size. Hence, light is not a quantity. Neither is it a body because two bodies cannot occupy the same space at the same time. But light and a transparent body can. Moreover, light cannot be a spirit, because we cannot sense spirits. But we can sense light. So, light must be something other than quantity, a body, or a spirit.

Mathematically, we cannot directly measure realities such as qualities, motions, time, actions, and so on, in the same way that we can directly compare the lengths of two pieces of wood by placing one next to or on top of another. The only reason we can compare and measure such realities is that, in some way, they exist in or cause measurable changes in bodies that have dimensions. Hence, analogously, we can say that we number, or measure, heat because heat causes mercury to react in a specific way within a numbered tube. Or we can compare weights by observing the effect they cause on a balance scale.

For such reasons, when we critically read a work in contemporary experimental science, we must be acutely aware of what we measure, the way we measure it, the experiments we conduct, and the way we employ measuring technologies and conduct experiments. Experiments are simply instances, or examples, of the mathematical formulas used as explanations of how to measure the realities in question.

Finally, when we read a mathematical work or a work in experimental science, the same general rules for critical reading apply as they do to the reading of any other work: (1) pay attention to the title, Table of Contents, sub-topics, definitions, examples, and so on, and, (2), from the start, construct a critical outline against the background of which to number the appearance of a book's contents to analyze into their most minute details.

Chapter 9

PHILOSOPHICALLY READING PRACTICAL MATTERS

A. Practical Definitions Make for Practical Reading

When I articulated specific guidelines for critically reading a book principally about theoretical matters, I made special note that the three general rules for philosophically reading any book apply to difficult readings in different ways. I indicated that definitions compose all difficult works written for enlightenment because all non-revelatory difficult works written for enlightenment set out to solve problems by proof. All proof involves using definitions because all proof involves using arguments. And all arguments involve applying definitions to a complex of examples. Hence, all difficult readings differ mainly in the definitions and examples that they apply in the arguments they use to solve their main problems.

In practical works, the main problems concern practical matters. Hence, the solutions they offer must involve practical definitions. What, however, is a practical definition? Since such a definition is part of the solution to a practical problem, to give a complete answer to this question, we need to understand the nature of a practical problem.

B. How We Define Practical Works

Like all problems, practical problems are difficulties. Only difficult things can be problems. Practical problems, therefore, are practical difficulties. At least two kinds of difficulties exist: (1) insurmountable (impossibilities), and (2) surmountable (possibilities that involve exerting some sort and degree of effort). Strictly speaking, practical problems are obstacles for which some finite possible solution exists. Obstacles that transcend the possibility of finite solution are mysteries, not finite practical problems. Practical problems must be practical obstacles amenable to possible finite solution. Obstacles are things that obstruct movement or action. Therefore, practical problems must obstruct practical finite movement or action, and must also be able to be removed from retarding such motion or action.

Strictly speaking, practical problems are, also, human problems. Just as theoretical problems are problems for human knowledge, so are practical ones. Just as we can solve theoretical problems by theoretical (observational) knowledge, so we can solve practical problems by practical (applied) knowledge. Practical knowledge is applicational, not observational. We achieve practical knowledge in the right exercise of human choice.

We always exercise choice with respect to the same specific object, the mature exercise of human action. Strictly speaking, human choice has only one specific object, maturely-exercised human action, healthy human acts. Specifically speaking, human beings can choose nothing else. For example, no human being chooses money, power, success, food, clothes, homes, automobiles, or any other sort of thing. We choose human acts and relations: to *possess* money, power, or success, to *buy* or *eat* food, to *buy* or *wear* clothes, to *mortgage* a home, to *drive* automobiles, and so on. In each instance, strictly speaking, we choose a maturely developed human action to which a thing relates as an enabling means. We can only choose the healthy exercise of own organic, facultative acts and relations. And we cannot exercise these acts and relations at all unless we employ maturely developed faculties and organs that we activate through contact with physical objects within our physical surroundings.

Properly speaking, then, to pose a practical problem for us, something must be an obstacle to the exercise of human choice. Exercise of human choice, however, depends upon the existence of several factors, including: (1) possession of healthy human faculties and organs (including intellect, will, memory, imagination, emotions, and external senses), (2) tools, (3) knowledge, (4) a goal, (5) time, (6) space, and (7) something that presents us with a problem of some magnitude through which to exercise a specific choice.

As Aristotle once noted, human choice is always of the humanly possible because it is always of the actual and for a means.[1] As living organic beings, actual objects of human choice exist in time and space, require that we use tools, and, as an act of choice, always demand that we possess knowledge and want to exercise human action. When we act out of ignorance and without desire, strictly speaking, we do not act out of choice. Moreover, since practical knowledge involves a practical problem, it includes confronting a problem that we have difficulty acting upon or moving. It must present us with a difficulty of some magnitude. Otherwise, it is not a problem for us.

A particular problem for our choice might not simply be a thing. It might simply be our surroundings, or some special weakness we have. For example, agent "A" might not be able to move thing "B" because thing is too big or heavy for agent "A" to handle. Agent "A ," however, might be seven years old; and thing "B" might be a sofa. Or agent "A" might be strong enough to move thing "B," but might not have enough time or space within which to move it. Hence, when determining the magnitude of a problem, we need to recognize that several things, other than the thing to be moved or acted upon, can cause a difficulty to be of some size or major proportion.

We define things in terms of how we generally identify them. Practical works that we read for understanding consider how to solve issues of some magnitude. We define all practical works in terms of the general nature of their activities and the magnitude of their difficulty regarding: (1) a particular agent with (2) limited abilities (3) acting upon some thing, (4) at a particular time and place, (5) under individual circumstances, (6) with limited means of availability, (7) in a definite order or sequence, (8) to construct a whole act, (9) by ordering partial actions through personal abilities and available tools, (10) in limited time and space, (11) within the context of other surrounding factors.

C. A Four-Step Approach to Reading a Practical Work

Since the definition of a practical problem involves many factors, critical readers must pay attention to the nature, motives, and circumstances of an action. We must consider who does what, to what, with what; what are the agent's natural and acquired abilities; what tools, how many, of what quality (including, where appropriate, friends, power, money, political/and other sorts, of influence) can that person utilize and how readily; how much time and space is available to an agent to resolve a problem; and how big is the problem in general and for this individual person especially.

Critical readers who read something for understanding and to solve a problem of major magnitude need to compare the attempted action to the agent within the context in which the action occurs. No human action happens in a vacuum. We always exercise choice in definite times and places, in relation to many surrounding actions within which a choice must be able to fit (such as, for example, weather conditions, hostile or friendly people or animals, and so on). Hence, when we try to solve a practical problem regarding farming or where to vacation, we need to consider who is the farmer or the vacationer and where, when, how, with what and so on.

To proceed in an orderly way to understand and solve a problem, we have to compare the agent to the contemplated action within the context in which the action is likely going to occur, and consider the action as means used progressively to reach a goal. A simple practical rule of thumb for resolving practical problems is a four-step approach: (1) identify the problem in terms of the magnitude of difficulty in kind and degree the thing being acted upon presents to anyone in general, and the agent in particular; (2) compare the nature and magnitude of the problem to the natural and acquired abilities of the agent seeking to undertake the action; (3) consider the likelihood of the agent's success or failure within the context of availability of time, space, and number and quality of outside forms of assistance (such as, the close availability of good and powerful tools, friends, and influence of different kinds, including numerous friends with skill and influence) and the possible need for good luck; and, (4), in estimating the likelihood of success or failure of the venture, view the potential action as a partial and smaller, present means within a progressively-developing whole resolution, and the resolution as a bigger, whole act being slowly constructed by smaller part-acts.

For example, consider a practical problem such as playing and winning a professional, championship football game. Playing this game is only one small part of the overall solution to the practical problem of organizing a football league of football teams; of practicing off season and winning in season; of getting advertisers, promoters, and media attention to generate fan interest; having times and locations to play, and professional quality equipment in sufficient quantity; coordinating travel plans; having the right weather conditions; having good coaches and trainers; having players with exceptional ability; avoiding injuries; and having luck on our side. Failure to take into consideration any one of these previous factors could spell the death of a season for a team. So could any number of related factors, such as failure to recognize that a complete and winning game is won progressively, step by step, by putting smaller plays together as parts of the whole solution of winning; and that the whole game is made up of all its plays of different sizes, or is the sum of all its rightly ordered parts, which, when rightly ordered, with luck on our side, are the means to winning the game.

When we read critically for practical understanding, we must pay special attention to the four factors I mention above. This is crucial when we do a general and specific reading and corresponding outline of a book. At these points, we first identify the problem, its magnitude, and its possibility of solution. In the specific reading, we start to look for definitions, examples, and proof. Practical definitions are sets of directions that relate to ordering action in time and space. Hence, they tell us specifically to do this first, this second, third, and so on, just as manufacturers do for customers when they diagram for them the steps they have to follow completely and successfully to assemble their products. Furthermore, just like theoretical examples, practical examples involve applying definitions, practical definitions. We apply practical definitions through step-by-step performance in space and time, such as assembling a table or hitting a baseball. The act of assembling the table and of hitting the baseball are the examples of the acts defined by the manufacturer and the coach. If the definition is true, it will specifically direct a person to order whole actions. All definitions identify wholes through the order of their parts. And, if the part acts directed to be done do identify the whole act, in practice, they will produce the whole act (or completed or finished product) by assembling its parts in the order directed.

This means that, in the third reading of a practical book, fully to judge it critically, we must understand and follow its directions in the most minute detail before being able to evaluate it as true or false, or good or bad. After they finish their reading, critical readers of theoretical books should be able to summarize these works succinctly. Analogously, critical readers of practical works should be able to put their directions into practice, at least, if the critical readers read the work for practical, not theoretical, reasons.

When we critically read a work for practical understanding, we must know what and why we are reading. This means that we must become familiar with the jargon used in different areas of practical reading, such as, in speech communication, computer science, economics, and politics. Moreover, should we encounter difficulty understanding the nature or given directions in practical action, some helpful things we can do are to: (1) consider the tools predominately used in an activity, (2) carefully observe their design, (3) and consider the agent who will apply these tools, under what conditions, in what order and way, to what part of what thing.

Economics is a good example of the utility of the above steps. Money is a primary tool of economic activity. As a tool, many people only think of money as a medium of exchange. It is much more. Consider any denomination of money: a penny, nickel, or dollar bill. These tools are mathematical measuring devices having the three general properties of all mathematical measures: equality, uniformity, and regularity. They are equal, uniform, and regular measures of something, with numbers stamped or engraved on them. Monetary denominations contain political symbols, thereby indicating a connection between money and political activity. Understandable, since money is a promissory note. Money is a contract to exchange that represents something to which a government bears witness: wealth. Money measures wealth. Wealth lies in possession of good tools for exercising human action, including intelligence and honesty. For this reason, trust in government must support money as a medium of exchange. If a government topples, a society's money becomes worthless. Media of exchange in the hands of fools are not measures of wealth. The commodities of which they supposedly represent possession are not securely held.

What is true of this example is true of every tool because every tool involves application of a definition. Hence, when we confront particular difficulties in reading, paying careful attention to the tools used can determine our success or failure to read a work critically.

Chapter 10

PHILOSOPHICALLY READING MATTERS OF IMAGINABLE EXPERIENCE

A. Imaginable Definitions Make for Imaginable Reading

When I started to identify the nature of reading, I noted how this activity never could have arisen unless people first had developed the ability to make sounds and draw or engrave. Reading presupposes (1) the ability to transfer some mental content, normally conveyed through sound, and represent it imaginatively and physically through figured, curved, and angled lines, and (2), in a way, to hear something through our eyes. Reading is a complicated act, involving numerous faculties, of which the ears are one, and not the most important. Strictly speaking, reading is possible because hearing is essentially a personal act, not an act of the ears. Since facultative acts are personal, when a sense faculty is impaired, such as in blindness, we can compensate for the deprivation of this faculty by more intense use of other faculties. We can even read with our fingers, even though this activity normally takes place through our ears.

This ability to transfer mental content through a wide variety of sensory means accounts for the origin of writing and reading and of incredible amounts and variety of arts and technology developed over the centuries. If we can transfer audible content through visual and imaginary lines, we can imagine the reverse to be possible, to transfer the mental content wrapped in visual and imaginary lines through sound. Our ability to use books to teach speech and music becomes an imaginable possibility, and an eventual reality. When we add to these abilities technologies that extend our voices over long distance (through wires at first, in the form of phone-writing, telegraph) and written letters through voice technologies (fax machines), we get some idea of how important is this transferability for the general progressive improvement of human learning and, especially, the ongoing growth of human inventiveness. By transferring sound we can create arts of body and foot movement such as dance and ballet.

I mention this transferability as a crucial factor in human learning and inventiveness because recognition of the existence of this process helps us understand how to read books about imaginable experiences. In these works, a similar kind of transfer takes place. Not of the content of sound into curved and angled, figured lines, but of any and every part of the physical universe and human experience into the quantified and qualified texture of the human imagination.

When we write works about imaginable experiences, we have to act somewhat like the historian and re-create events. Imaginative writers are not as strictly bound by the order of spatial and temporal appearance of past events, or the causal connections that generated them, as they are by the natures of things. Given certain images, ideas, and emotions with which to work, abstracted from the real world in which we live, we can re-assemble these materials in mostly any fashion reason and imagination can envision.

We cannot completely divorce our mental content from the material things from which they are abstracted. To some extent, imaginative writers cannot define the characters and settings of an imaginary time and place in so free a fashion that they bear no generic and specific resemblance to characters and settings of real times and places. Still, given these essential materials, we are largely free to assemble these as we see fit.

A main difference between an imaginative writer and other writers is the primary subject of concern with which each deals.

Strictly speaking, in all the other difficult books we have examined, the problems studied have related primarily to publicly experiencable realities, not to privately experienced psychological states. All other books tell stories about individual realities, the individual natures of which, in some way, do, did, can, could, will, might, or should exist outside our faculties and organs. The worlds of the imaginative writer consist, mainly, of personal psychic realities, such as ideas, images, volitions, and emotions, that we try skillfully to arrange in different ways to convey to a reader something about our private experience to which a reader has no other way to gain something resembling public access. While other writers convey information about, and through real, natural and artificial, publicly experiencable wholes and definitions, imaginative authors convey information through and about privately experienced, imaginary, artificial wholes.

This means is that, in the most complete sense, the materials and tools upon, and, with which, the imaginative author works are principally imaginatively re-constructed ideas, images, and emotions. Hence, unlike the historian, when the imaginative author tells a story about a historical event, such as the assassination of John F. Kennedy, the object of the imaginative author's speculation is the historical character and events as imagined, not the historical character and events as such. Through imaginative re-creation of characters and events we seek to convey an accurate and precise recreation of personal, imaginative, emotional and volitional experiences, not an accurate and precise knowledge of history. Imaginative writers paint and orchestrate characters and events to enable readers, analogously, to share in a personal, appetitive event, not to comprehend a historical occurrence.

In this respect, all imaginative works resemble practical, or how to, books. Just as how to books give us a set of directions and steps to explain how to assemble some physical object, imaginative books lead us through sequential steps of imagining things to be in a certain way to cause us to experience some kind and intensity of emotional and volitional experience. A love poem, for example, assembles words in order and rhyme to create an emotion-laden image to replicate in a reader the emotional and volitional intensity an author has experienced.

Imaginable definitions are artificial, abstracted and reshaped from the natures of things to convey an anomalous content: an additional imaginatively-constructed and emotionally-associated message.

To understand such definitions more precisely, recall that, in the last chapter, I mentioned that the three general rules for reading any book apply to difficult readings in different ways. And I said that definitions compose all difficult works written for enlightenment because such difficult works attempt to solve problems by logical proof. All such proof involves use of definitions because all logical proof involves use of arguments. And all arguments involve applying definitions to a complex of examples. Consequently, all problematic, but understandable, readings differ mainly in the definitions and examples that they apply in the arguments they use to solve their main problems.

The main problems in imaginable works often concern matters that defy theoretical and practical public scrutiny because the information they seek to convey is a problematic, privately experienced, emotional and volitional state. Imaginable works consider personal, emotional and volitional obstacles and conflicts that we try to recreate and share with others through the way we imaginatively construct characters, events, and scenes and organize and develop them through word formation. Hence, the solutions that such works offer must involve use of imaginable definitions.

But, what is an imaginable definition? Since such a definition is part of the solution to a imaginable problem, we must understand the nature of a imaginable problem.

B. How We Define Imaginable Works

To grasp the nature of an imaginable problem, we need to notice something about the way we can transfer information through alternative and reconstructed personal routes. Just as audible words were first transferred to written ones through engraving and painting, so we can engrave and paint a picture through words and images. Through words, we can symbolize our private psychic content, including our knowledge of the world we share with other organic beings and our emotional and volitional experiences.

Words are tools for transporting information, physical realities and symbols. As physical realities, they can have many uses, including being political weapons and causes of physical benefit or damage. As symbols of information and of emotional engagement, and as simple physical realities, words can help and hurt. For example, when our hearing is damaged by someone shouting into our ears.

As physical, words cause sensibility, images, and emotion. Different sights and sounds of varying intensity and organization cause pleasure and pain, enjoyment and irritation. As symbols, words can convey images and emotions when we associate them with people and situations that involve imaginable and emotional content. And images can generate emotional states within us. No emotional state emerges without an image. And we can alter the state to the extent that we intensify, diminish, or replace the image.

The skilled, imaginative author is aware of these qualities of words, symbols, images, colors, sounds, emotions, and so on. These are tools of the trade. Hence, such an artist is much like a painter who seeks to share a personal experience with others but who uses the organization of words, images, and their emotional and volitional associations to get the message across.

We primarily define imaginable works, therefore, in terms of the complexity and intensity of the volitional and emotional experience that we wish to convey. As imaginative authors, our main problem is how to convey complicated and intense, personal, and non-physically observable, experiences by physical tools. Without using physical symbols (words, gestures, honors, poems, rings, cards, flowers, and so on), we have no way to convey information about our psychic experiences to other people. Physical objects become symbols precisely when they start to bear intellectual, emotional, and volitional content. Hence, as part of their nature as imaginable and great, great imaginable works are intensely symbolic.

We may write imaginable works for practical or theoretical reasons. Included within our main purpose of sharing personal experience, we might have a goal to teach a moral or political lesson, or the simple contemplative appreciation and enjoyment of something beautiful. As such, our imaginative works can be imaginable, practical, and theoretical. Every imaginable work has to be principally one or the other.

C. How to Read Imaginable Works

Because imaginable definitions and examples compose every imaginable work, and because such works are practical or theoretical, when we read an imaginable work, we must constantly watch for imaginable, theoretical and practical definitions and examples. Imaginable definitions are part of the solution to imaginable problems. And imaginable problems always relate to our emotions and choice. Hence, when we read books about imaginable experience for enlightenment, we need to look for situations of intense emotional or volitional conflict, and understand some things about our emotions and acts of choice.

All emotions are psychosomatic reactions of living, organic, temporal and spatial, environmental beings to things that influence our operation and survival. All our emotions relate to, and cannot be understood apart from, human choice. Choice, however, is always of an individual, actual, possible, temporal and spatial means. We always make a choice by comparing the magnitude of our natural and acquired abilities to the magnitude of difficulty of the thing to be moved or acted upon, within our surrounding context of place, time, opportunity, access and availability of tools, and natural agents. Furthermore, choice is always a movement toward exercising human action in relation to something that we imagine we love or like as a human being.

We always generate emotions in relation to something that we imagine we like or love in relation to our suspected ability to execute or enjoy a human action in individual situations. Strictly speaking, only one human emotion exists, love or liking. All other emotions are species of this one general emotion that we generate in relation to the way we consider what we like or love as accessible within a specific context. For example, if we like something in the present, actually possess it, picture it imaginatively as so possessed, and realize it as possessed, we experience pleasure.

If, on the other hand, because of remoteness in time or space, we do not have an object of love, then the object moves us to *love after*, or desire to get, it. If some formidable, but manageable, obstacles stand in the way of our future acquisition of such objects, then our desire extends into the area of future possibility. We call this longing to overcome such manageable difficulties "hope." And we activate hope by picturing our ability of overcome the obstacles. We can produce this hope by anything that can help us imagine ourselves able to overcome a personal obstacle (natural and/or acquired abilities, easy temporal and spatial accessibility of powerful tools, many friends of intense power and influence, money, extensive amounts of time and space available to work, or even alcoholism, our own stupidity, or youthful naivete).

When we face a formidable obstacle we seek to overcome, we define all our emotions in reference to love considered as hope. Hence, when, for one reason or another, we start to imagine an obstacle as too difficult to overcome, hope starts to approach despair through growing frustration. In the face of the reasonable estimate of our ability to overcome personal danger and the combined readiness to attack the danger, hope takes on the form of courage. The suspicion of inability to overcome personal obstacles to achieve what we hope for, in turn, leads to hope's contrary, fear. In the face of fear of work, when we unreasonably estimate work to be too difficult, fear is, specifically, laziness. In the face of formidable danger, such irrational fear is cowardice. In relation to the irrational fear of losing a loved one, fear is called "jealousy." And, finally, hope in the face of getting revenge for being subjected to unjust damage is anger. All these emotions can be, and are, altered in relation to imagined possibilities of altering conditions of time, space, opportunity to act, power of the agent, and suspicion of one's own strength.

Given the extensive influence that human choice, emotions, and difficulty play in imaginable works, when we read such books, we must define the work's problem in terms of factors related to hope. Only formidable obstacles, imagined as formidable, generate the intensity of emotion and will demanded of great imaginable works. Great works of fiction, poetry, music, painting, sculpture, and drama composed for enlightenment all deal with sharing intense emotional and volitional experiences by weaving together imaginary scenes in which we define such emotions and volitions in terms of characters, or material, reflecting formidable obstacles, that test human ability, and define the character or material as an example of an emotional lesson to be conveyed or from which to learn.

When we read an imaginable work, such as drama, for enlightenment, we must use all the rules and skills already mentioned related to theoretical and practical readers, and add to these a keen awareness of character-development and the above psychology of the human emotions and human choice. As always, we must hunt for definitions and examples. But we must be conscious of relating these to the nature of obstacle that a character confronts and the attendant emotions that this confrontation generates. When we read works like poetry for enlightenment, instead of enjoyment, we need to define the problem in terms of the sections of the poem. We need to analyze words carefully in reference to the work's title and the poem's layout. In addition, to familiarize ourselves with reading poetry, we need to outline the poem. And, if need be, even to rewrite it, in simple sentences.

To literary purists, this last suggestion might sound shocking. It should not. Reading is a kind of listening. And poetry is primarily meant to be spoken, not read. To read it as conveying an author's thought, emotion, or volition, we must understand it, and to understand it, we must hear and comprehend the words as the author intends us to hear them. A shallow emotional and intellectual appreciation of a great poetic work does no justice to the author or the reader. In such a reading of a great work, we delight in our sense of confusion and ignorance of what the author intends, not in our knowledge of what the author says.[1]

Chapter 11

PHILOSOPHICALLY READING MIXED MATTERS

A. What is a Work Involving Mixed Matters?

Above, I have distinguished and examined four general types of books according to their importance. I have explained the respective methods we need to practice to read each of these philosophically. To consider what we need to do to read a work involving mixed matters is somewhat superfluous. I have already given all the necessary information.

Still, to some extent, all difficult reading material involves practical or theoretical matters. And we tend to read all books for information, understanding, and enjoyment. Hence, no book is completely unmixed with respect to importance of subject matter and motives for reading.

While all difficult works might be somewhat mixed, an author has always had some predominant object of concern in view when writing a book. And a reader has some main motive for reading it. Consequently, properly speaking, to some extent, we can accurately identify all commonly read, difficult books as (1) predominantly theoretical or practical, (2) about matters of measurement, or (3) about imaginable experiences. And all mixed books concern one or more of these three categories. For example, some books are principally practical works, concerned with matters of measurement, read primarily for understanding. Others are mainly theoretical works, about imaginable experiences, read primarily for sharing intensity of personal emotion.

B. A Few Suggestions for Reading a Work Involving Mixed Matters

Aside from all the information I have given in the previous chapters, philosophically to read a work involving mixed matters demands that we identify with precision which kind of matter predominates in the work, and our main motives for reading. For example, does the author mainly intend the work as theoretical or practical? Am I reading it mainly for a practical or theoretical motive? Am I primarily reading to understand what the author says, or to share in some intense personal experience that the author intends to convey?

With these notions clarified, when we outline and apply our outline to the work, as precisely as possible, we need to delineate where specific topics of concern within the text change from being theoretical to practical, from about matters of fact to matters of imaginable experience, from being read for theoretical or practical understanding, or for sharing an intense personal experience, and so on. Then, within the different sections, we need to outline each appropriately (according to its distinctive subject matter and methods), and pay attention to the sorts of definitions, examples, and arguments with which we deal in respective parts of the work. Finally, we need to employ these definitions, examples, and arguments to understand the work as a whole in light of the most precise comprehension of the most minute details of its various parts.

CONCLUSION

Philosophical reading is a skill that we acquire through continual practice and hard work. It offers great rewards. Especially for an avid reader, the effort is minimal. If we intend to read difficult works to understand what they say, in the long run, the effort we exert to read them philosophically is significantly less than we exert to read them weakly and uncritically.

In this book, I give readers guidelines for skillful, philosophical reading that, from thirty years of college and university teaching, with thousands of students of differing intellectual abilities, from all backgrounds, and settings, I know are highly effective in removing obstacles to independently learning even the most difficult matters. I have derived this method of reading from my practice of studying medieval texts and observing the way in which medieval commentators used philosophical reading skills within their research. These techniques are effective because: (1) they are philosophically rigorous, and (2) they follow the natural way in we are inclined to discover things on our own by first becoming familiar with objects in general before trying to understand them in detail.

In my opinion, the main obstacle to becoming highly educated is not, in general, that people cannot think critically (in the sense that they are generally unable to follow logical reasoning when we clearly and precisely present it to them). It is not that the content of works dealing with major intellectual discoveries transcends the comprehension of most normal human beings. The main obstacle to achieving higher education is to misunderstand the nature of that obstacle itself! In general, this obstacle is that people do not possess the art of critical, or philosophical, reading. No matter how intelligent some people might be in understanding their respective subject matters, most of us, college and non-college educated, are weak and unphilosophical readers. Our main mistake is to try "to put the cart before the horse."

The main reason we tend to remain weak readers is that we do not realize we put the cart before the horse. As a result, in reading a difficult work, instead of attempting to read in an orderly, logical, and philosophically skillful way from general to particular and detailed familiarity, we try to read without any such game plan, and naively expect to be able immediately and completely to understand the precise details of a subject with which we have little general familiarity. No one can read skillfully in this way, no matter how natively intelligent we might think we are, and no matter where we might have been educated.

Nevertheless, an "art" of critical reading does exist. Schoolmen of the late Middle Ages first developed it when they started to read by writing commentaries on philosophical works. I have included the essential elements of this method of philosophical reading in this book. Just as the ancient Greeks partly developed philosophy as a skill of *critical conversation*, because they lacked the extensive art of writing, so Medieval scholastics developed philosophy as a skill of critical reading because they were unable to engage great thinkers of the" past in such critical conversation so as to learn from them. In this way, they could introduce many classroom students to philosophical conversation with the great thinkers of the past.

If an average reader consistently applies the directions I give to read great books (works that great discoverers of the past and present have traditionally read), no reason exists why any average person cannot enter this tradition of the Medieval Schoolmen and become masterful and critical thinkers and develop the ability to become great, independent discoverers.

This handbook is a powerful learning tool. By means of it, we can enter the greatest of universities and obtain the best and highest of all educations, at virtually no cost and no entrance requirements, other than to put into practice the advice contained herein.

If we practice reading works that are over our heads (especially, books that have stood the test of time as "great") using the techniques recommended in this book, then we enter into philosophical conversation with, and learn under direction of, the greatest discoverers of all time. The test of time bears witness to the greatness of these people's intellects because human beings tend to discard junk, especially when it is difficult to keep. Great books are intellectual heirlooms, the most prized intellectual possessions of generations of people.

To be able to access the contents of such prized possessions is a pearl of great price. By gaining entrance to philosophical conversation with the greatest discoverers of the past, we become students of the greatest of teachers, and get the greatest education accessible to anyone. These greatest discoverers are the most scientific and wisest of all human beings. The key to the entrance of this door of highest education, and, therefore, to science and wisdom, lies in the hands of the philosophical reader. You hold this key in your hands. Whether you use it is now is up to you.

QUESTIONS FOR STUDY AND DISCUSSION

Introduction

A.

1. What do we mean by the term "to read"?

2. What makes anything difficult?

3. What is a book?

4. What makes books difficult to read?

B.

1. Do you think we have an illiteracy problem today? If so, why?

2. Is it possible for us to read the thoughts of another person? If so, how? 3. What are words? Are words identical with sounds?

4. Is an image identical with an idea? If not, how do they differ?

5. What do we mean by the term "liberal arts"?

C.

1. Are learning and knowing identical?

2. Can we learn without knowing?

3. Can we know without learning?

4. What is the difference between teaching and learning?

5. Can we learn without teaching?

6. Can we teach without learning?

7. What is the difference between a discovery and invention?

8. What are tools?

9. What makes one tool better than another?

10. How is reading related to tools?

11. What is a culture?

12. Can cultures exist without reading?

13. Can reading exist without cultures?

14. As precisely you can, outline this Introduction.

Chapter 1

A.

1. Is learning different from experience? If so, how?

2. Before reading exists in a culture, who is likely to be the leading teacher?

3. Can reading damage a culture's progress?

4. Can people be illiterate but intelligent?

5. When we design tools well, what do we have to take into consideration?

B.

1. What is work?

2. What is leisure?

3. Do thieves work?

4. Can we work without tools?

5. What do we mean by the term "use"?

6. What does it mean to use a tool?

7. What is language?

8. How is language related to intellectual development?

9. What do we mean by the term "to write"?

10. Can we write without reading?

C.

1. What is a poet?

2. Why are poets important to cultural development?

3. What do we mean by the term "to listen"?

4. How can sounds have length?

5. If sounds have no length, can we have words?

6. What is a conversation?

D.

1. What do we mean by "power"?

2. Can something be powerful but not good?

3. Can something be good but not powerful? .

4. What is the imagination?

5. How is the imagination related to language development?

6. Can some languages be better than others? If so, why and how?

7. As precisely you can, outline Chapter 1.

Chapter 2

A.

1. What do we mean by a thing's purpose?

2. Can a thing have a purpose without having a use?

3. Can a thing have a use without having a purpose?

4. What is an emotion?

5. Can we have emotions without images?

6. Can we have emotions without knowledge?

7. Can we have knowledge or images without emotion?

8. What do we mean by the term "enjoyment"?

9. What do we mean by information?

B.

1. What do we mean when we say that one thing is "more" or "less" than another?

2. Can two things be equal without being one?

3. Can two things be one without being equal?

4. Can two things be equal without being the same?

5. Can two things be the same without being equal?

6. Can two things be different if they are in no way the same?

7. Can something be great (or have magnitude) without being numerically large?

8. Can one color be brighter than another without being greater than another?

9. Is effort the same as work?

10. What do we mean by practice?

11. Why does practice make us familiar with doing things?

C.

1. Can we learn without being liberal artists?

2. Can we be liberal artists without being lemurs?

3. What is a habit?

4. Can we have skills without habits?

5. Can we have habits without skills?

6. How are our images and emotions related to our skills?

7. How are liberal arts skills?

8. How does language develop from sounds?

9. How does reading develop from hearing?

D.

1. What is an alphabet?

2. How do alphabets first develop?

3. Can people with no knowledge of geometry develop alphabets?

4. How is imaginative development related to language development?

5. What is wisdom?

6. How is reading related to wisdom?

7. How is teaching related to books?

8. Can different types of teaching exist? If so, what are they?

9. What enables us to distinguish one book from another?

10. What makes a book great?

11. As precisely as you can, outline Chapter 2.

Chapter 3

A.

1. How does the way we learn relate to the way we differentiate books?

2. What is teaching?

3. What enables us to distinguish one thing from another?

4. Do different ways of teaching exist? If so, how do we distinguish them?

5. What is a seminar? Why are some classes taught in seminars while others are not?

B.

1. What is definition? Explain.

2. What is an explanation? Explain.

3. If truth does not exist, can teachers exist?

4. How is reading related to the liberal arts?

5. As precisely as you can, outline Chapter 3.

Chapter 4

A.

1. What do we mean by the question "What?"?

2. What makes a teacher great?

3. Identify several liberal arts subjects, and explain how we teach liberal arts.

4. What is the difference between something theoretical and practical?

B.

1. How is powerful and critical reading a liberal art?

2. What is the difference between a real whole and an imaginary whole?

3. What is the difference between an artificial whole and a real whole?

4. What do we mean when we call something a "symbol"?

5. As precisely as you can, outline Chapter 4

Chapter 5

A.

1. What makes a person a powerful and critical reader?

2. What does it mean to "measure" something?

3. On the basis of subjects studied, what is the most general division we can make about books?

4. Why do powerful and critical readers have to think about the nature of the book they will read before they start to read it?

B.

1. What is a fact?

2. Can an opinion be a fact? Is your opinion about your answer to this question a fact? Yes or No, and why?

3. How do imaginable experience differ from real ones?

4. How is opinion different from certainty?

C.

1. Can people be certain of anything? Explain. Are you certain? Explain.

2. What is the difference between certainty and doubt?

3. How is doubt different from opinion?

4. Is science the same as certainty?

D.

1. Can we have science without certainty?

2. Can we have certainty without science?

3. What is a rule?

4. Can something be a rule without being a measure?

E.

1. Can something be a measure without being a rule?

2. What rules, if any, do you think that people need to follow to be powerful and critical readers?

3. What is an outline? Why do people use outlines?

4. As precisely as you can, outline Chapter 5.

Chapter 6

A.

1. What is a conversation?

2. In what way is a book always a conversation?

3. To follow a complicated conversation, what do we have to do?

4. What can we do when we read to help locate difficult and important information?

B.

1. Can we read and understand difficult books without using numbers? Explain.

2. Can we gradually increase our knowledge of anything difficult without, at first, being generally familiar with what we find difficult?

3. How do we rationally decrease the difficulty of anything we try to understand?

4. What does it mean "order" something?

5. Can we order anything without, in some way, numbering it?

C.

1. What is a rational argument?

2. What do we have to do to follow a complicated argument?

3. Why do we call an outline an "outline"?

4. Why do we call a Table of Contents a "table"?

D.

1. What is the difference between a sentence outline and a topic outline?

2. Can we make a sentence outline without making a topic outline?

3. Can we make a topic outline without making a sentence outline?

4. What kinds of topics comprise a difficult hook?

5. What do we mean when we say that we know something "precisely"?

6. What, if anything, prevents us from knowing something precisely?

E.

1. Can we know something precisely without first knowing it vaguely? Explain precisely.

2. What enables us to read something precisely?

3. What differentiates one kind of reading from another?

F.

1. What is the difference between knowing something theoretically and practically?

2. Are historical works theoretical or practical?

3. Is mathematics theoretical or practical?

4. Do a topic and sentence outline of Chapter 6.

Chapter 7

A.

1. What do we mean when we say we "prove" something?

2. Is it possible to prove anything without using definitions?

3. What do we mean when we say we have a "motive" for doing something?

B.

1. What differences do books have that enable us to define books in different ways?

2. What differences do we have that enable us to define books in different ways?

3. Can something be past and not be historical? Explain.

4. Is history a science? an art? neither? Explain.

C.

1. How is a historical work different from a dramatic work?

2. Are theoretical works theoretical or practical? Explain.

3. How do contemporary philosophical works differ from ancient philosophical writings?

4. Can a mathematical work be a historical work?

5. How do mathematical works differ from historical works?

6. Why do people measure things?

7. What do we mean by the term "to measure"?

8. How do we measure things?

9. How are measures useful to us?

D.

1. Why do we need measures to be uniform?

2. What is quantity?

3. Can something non-physical have quantity?

4. What do we mean when we say something is "one."[?]

5. What do we mean by the term "to number"?

6. Can we measure things without numbering them?

7. Can we number things without measuring them?

8. Can motion have length? size? If so, how?

9. Do historians measure things. If so, what?

10. Do a topic and sentence outline of Chapter 7.

Chapter 8

A.

1. How do mathematical ideas differ from other ideas?

2. From where do we first get mathematical ideas?

3. What is a point?

4. Can lines exits if points don't exist? Can points exist if lines don't exist?

B.

1. What is a surface?

2. How do we measure surfaces?

3. Can volumes exist if surfaces don't exist? Can surfaces exist if volumes don't exist?

4. How do we measure volumes? Why?

C.

1. Is heat a quantity? Does it have size?

2. Is it possible to measure qualities? If so, where do we get our measures of quality?

3. Is it possible to measure beauty? If so, where do we get our measures of beauty?

4. Who were Galileo Galilei and Sir Isaac Newton?

5. What role did Galileo and Newton play in the development of modern science?

6. How is a measuring scientist like a fiction writer?

D.

1. Why do we use different types of measuring devices for measuring different things?

2. How do we measure weight? time? speed? a healthy heart? Why?

E.

1. What makes mathematical books difficult to read?

2. How can we simplify our reading of mathematical works?

F.

1. What makes books about experimental science difficult to read?

2. How can we simplify our reading of books about experimental science?

3. How do we arrive at practical definitions?

4. How do practical and theoretical definitions differ?

5. Is modern experimental science theoretical or practical? Explain.

6. Do a topic and sentence outline of Chapter 8.

Chapter 9

A.

1. How does a theoretical problem differ from a practical problem?

2. What is choice?

3. What faculties do we always use when we make choices?

4. What conditions facilitate our ability to make choices? Why?

5. What conditions weaken our ability to make choices? Why?

6. What conditions must be present for us to be able to make choices?

7. How do we define practical works?

B.

1. In general, what elements do we use to define things?

2. What makes a definition good or bad?

3. How do we test definitions? Why?

4. What makes a practical work difficult?

5. What is an effective way to read a difficult practical work for

understanding?

C.

1. In solving practical problems, do we use our imaginations in the same that we do when we solve theoretical problems? Explain.

2. To imagine a practical problem, what do we have to do?

3 When we imagine things, where do we get the information that we use in our images?

4. Are some things always necessary to do when we solve practical problems? If so, what are they?

5. Do a topic and sentence outline of Chapter 9.

Chapter 10

A.

1. What is the main difference between an imaginable and real experience? Explain.

2. What is an imaginable problem? Explain.

3. What is an imaginable definition? Explain.

4. How do we define imaginable works? Explain.

B.

1. What is an emotion?

2. How do emotions relate to imaginable works?

3. Can we like something without hoping for it?

4. Can we hope for something without liking it?

5. Can we experience pleasure without fear?

6. Can we experience fear without pleasure?

7. If something cannot hurt us, can we fear it?

8. If something can do us no good can we like, or hope for, it?

9. Can a person be courageous without being hopeful?

10. Can a person be hopeful without being courageous?

11. Can a person with no awareness of time be hopeful?

12. Can a person fear without hope?

13. Can a person hope without fear?

14. Can we choose something we in no way like?

15. Can we like something without choosing it?

C.

1. How do we imagine emotions?

2. What do we mean when we call something "intense."[?]

3. Can something be beautiful without, in some way, being great.

4. Can something be great without being beautiful?

5. What makes anything beautiful?

6. What makes a work of art "art"?

7. What makes a work of art a "work"?

8. What makes a work of art beautiful?

9. What makes imaginable works difficult to read?

10. How do we read a difficult imaginable work for understanding?

11. Do a topic and sentence outline of Chapter 10.

Chapter 11

A.

1. How can we read for understanding a theoretical, practical, imaginable book?

B.

1. What is philosophical reading?

2. How is philosophical reading related to "higher" education?

3. Do a topic and sentence outline of Chapter 11.

Conclusion

1. In one or a few sentences, summarize this subject of this book.

2. Do you think this is a good book? Defend your answer.

3. Do a topic and sentence outline of Chapter 11.

NOTES

Introduction

[1] Mortimcr J. Adler, *How to Read a Book* (London: Jarrolds Publishers, Ltd., 1949), 11.

[2] *Ibid.*, 43.

[3] *Ibid.*, 45.

[4] *Ibid.*, 39.

[5] *Ibid.*, 41–42.

[6] *Ibid.*, 43.

[7] *Ibid.*

[8] *Ibid.*, 38.

[9] I think Gilson says this in *Thomist Realism and the Critique of Knowledge* or in *Methodical Realism*.

[10] Mortimer J. Adler, *How to Read a Book*, 9–51.

[11] See Mortimer J. Adler and Charles Van Doren, *How to Read a Book: The Classic Guide to Intelligent Reading* (New York: Simon and Schuster, 1972).

[12] Mortimer J. Adler, *How to Read a Book*, 45.

Chapter 1

[1] Mortimer J. Adler, *How to Read a Book*, 24–29.

²On the basis of this distinction, Socrates always claimed never to be a teacher. He did this because, during his time, the ancient Greeks generally thought learning to be a passive state in which a person was filled by inspiration through revelation from the gods. The ancient poets, especially, apparently popularized this view, which Socrates severely criticized in such works of Plato as the *Meno* and the *Phaedo*.

³Adler makes this helpful distinction in, *How to Read a Book*, 29–31.

⁴My own views about the nature of tools synthesize several sources, including Plato, Aristotle, Aquinas, Yves R. Simon, and McLuhan. For McLuhan's perceptive observations about tools, see Marshall McLuhan, *Understanding Media: The Extensions of Man* (New York and Scarborough, Ontario: New American Library). Regarding Simon, see his *Work, Society, and Culture*, ed. Vukan Kuic (New York: Fordham University Press, 1971).

⁵I develop my views about the way figures trap sound from the work of Charles B. Crowley, Aquinas's faculty psychology, Plato's doctrine of recollection, and McLuhan, *Understanding Media: The Extensions of Man*, 81–114.

⁶See Adler, *How to Read a Book*, 16–29

⁷Marshall McLuhan, *Understanding Media: The Extensions of Man*, 145–150 and 155–162.

⁸*Ibid.*, 106–114. See, also, Jorge J. E. *Gracia, Philosophy and Its History: Issues in Philosophical Historiography* (State University of New York Press, 1992).

Chapter 2

¹I follow Plato, Aristotle, Aquinas, and Adler in making this distinction. Adler appears to follow Socrates' original distinction about three different kinds of human good (*Republic*, Book II)

and Aristotle's famous distinction among theoretical, practical, and productive ways of knowing. Adler realizes that reading is a kind of listening, but I derive the implications from this fact that Adler does not. See Adler, *How to Read a Book*, 16–29.

²Mortimer J. Adler, *How to Read a Book*, 29–37. For a more extensive treatment of Adler's views on learning see his *Reforming Education: The Opening of the American Mind*, ed. Geraldine Van Doren (New York: Macmillan Publishing Company and London: Collier Macmillan Publishers, 1988).

³Aristotle, *Metaphysics*, 980b–981 a.

⁴Marshall McLuhan, *Understanding Media: The Extensions of Man*, 81–90 and 106–114.

⁵For more about the liberal arts, see E. R. Curtius, *European Literature and the Latin Middle Ages*, trans. Willard R. Trask (New York: Pantheon Books, Bollingen Series, XXXVI, 1948).

⁶I am not sure that Adler uses these words as I have italicized them. I drew this conclusion after reading pages 163–190 of his *How to Read a Book*.

⁷I analogously transfer to reading a frequently used metaphysical principle of Aristotle and Aquinas that a little bit of knowledge of divine things is worth much more than extensive amounts of knowledge of lesser things.

Chapter 3

¹Mortimer J. Adler, *How to Read a Book*, 52–59.

²*Ibid.*, 35.

³*Ibid.*, 33–35.

⁴*Ibid.*, 35.

⁵*Ibid.*

⁶This same reasoning appears to lie at the base of Adler's emphasis upon the need to read "Great Books" to become highly educated.

Chapter 4

¹In part, this general division of books is similar to Adler's. I take parts from him, just as he does from Aristotle. However, my division, and the metaphysical views behind them, widely differ from Adler's.

Chapter 5

¹In general, I give the same recommendation to a reader as Adler about how to approach a book. From this point on, our views tend to diverge dramatically. I think Adler unnecessarily complicates the critical reading process by improperly understanding the role played by the *quadrivium* in developing communications arts and by failing to realize that critical reading is more than a liberal art: a philosophical activity.

Chapter 6

¹Aquinas also quite dramatically realized this point about ideas. For example, see Armand A. Maurer's translation of Questions *Five and Six of St. Thomas's commentary on Boethius's de Trinitate*, entitled *The Division and Methods of the Sciences* (Toronto: Pontifical Institute of Mediaeval Studies, 1963), especially Question VI, a. 2, 68–72.

²See Gilson's *Thomist Realism and the Critique of Knowledge* and his *Methodical Realism*.

Chapter 7

[1] Luigi Guicciardini, *The Sack of Rome*, ed. and trans. James H. McGregor (New York: Italica Press, 1993). See, especially, 1–60.

[2] In *How to Read a Book*, Adler also notes this dramatic character of historians. See, 136–143.

[3] David Hume, *An Inquiry Concerning Human Understanding*, ed. Charles W. Hendel (Indianapolis and New York: The Bobbs-Merrill Company, Inc., 1955), 40.

Chapter 8

[1] For more on this history of measurement and the nature of modern experimental science as a philosophy of measure, see a short history of measuring systems put out by the United States Department of Commerce, reprint of Special Publication 304A (revised August 1981), and Charles B. Crowley, *Aristotelian-Thomistic Philosophy of Measure and the International System of Units* (SI), ed. with a prescript by Peter A. Redpath (Lanham, Md.: University Press of America, 1996).

[2] *Ibid.*

[3] *Ibid.*, viii–xli.

[4] Pierre Conway, *Faith Views the Universe: A Thomistic Perspective*, ed. Mary Michael Spangler (Lanham, Md.: University Press of America, 1997), 31–66.

[5] Crowley, *Aristotelian-Thomistic Philosophy of Measure and the International System of Units* (SI), viii–xli.

Chapter 9

[1] My reasoning in this part of the text is largely derived from reflections upon Socrates' behavior in Plato's dialogues, Aristotle's treatment of choice in his *Nicomachean Ethics* and *Rhetoric*, Aquinas's analysis of the human emotions in different parts of the *Summa Theologiae*, and Yves R. Simon's writings about work.

Chapter 10

[1] See Charles B. Crowley, *Aristotelian-Thomistic Philosophy of Measure and the International System of Units* (SI), ed. Peter A. Redpath (Lanham, Md.: University Press of America, 1996).

Chapter 11

[1] Adler had noticed that reading skills developed during the high Middle Ages of the twelfth and thirteenth centuries were the basis of his teaching about reading (See *How to Read a Book*, 50). The thinkers who developed these techniques were great Scholastics, like St. Albert the Great and St. Thomas Aquinas, who applied philosophical reading within the context of their own disciplines of study to enter into conversations with, and learn from, great thinkers of antiquity. Despite this fact, and that, more than anything else, Adler would probably consider himself to be a philosopher and a Scholastic, Adler apparently never realized that critical reading is a philosophical skill, not simply a liberal art. The reason for this is, perhaps, Adler's mistaken identification of the traditional liberal arts with the *trivium* and his tendency to view philosophy as a logical *system*. The notion that philosophy is a *system* is modern, not ancient or medieval. (See Armand A. Maurer. *The Unity of a Science: St. Thomas and the Nominalists*, in *St. Thomas Aquinas, 1274–1974, Commemorative Studies*, ed. Armand A. Maurer, editor-in-chief., (Toronto: Pontifical Institute of Mediaeval Studies, 1974), Vol. 2, 269–291). Hence, the late medieval scholastic way of philosophizing was to engage great

thinkers of the past in critical, or philosophical, conversation through critical reading of books, not to create a system of ideas. They did this through written commentaries. For this reason, and not simply because they had a liberal art of reading, they "could read better than the best readers today" (*How to Read a Book*, 50). Moreover, despite his brilliance, because Adler failed to realize this philosophical dimension to critical reading, Adler's work in this area is unnecessarily prolix. His views about reading lack a philosophical unity that would have allowed him to express his thoughts more simply, uniformly, and completely.

www.ingramcontent.com/pod-product-compliance
Lightning Source LLC
Chambersburg PA
CBHW070909080526
44589CB00013B/1234